Taking Advantage of Media

Taking Advantage of Media

A manual for parents and teachers

Laurene Krasny Brown

ROUTLEDGE & KEGAN PAUL
Boston, London and Henley

First published in 1986
by Routledge & Kegan Paul plc
9 Park Street, Boston, Mass. 02108, USA

14 Leicester Square, London WC2H 7PH, England and

Broadway House, Newtown Road,
Henley on Thames, Oxon RG9 1EN, England

Set in Palatino and Rockwell
by Columns of Reading
and printed in Great Britain
by The Thetford Press Ltd
Thetford, Norfolk

Library of Congress Cataloging in Publication Data

Brown, Laurene Krasny.

Taking advantage of media.
Bibliography: p.
Includes index.
1. Audio-visual education. 2. Audio-visual
materials—Evaluation. I. Title.
LB1043.B755   1986   371.3'3   85-19601

British Library CIP data also available

ISBN 0-7102-0402-7

Contents

Foreword

by Howard Gardner

In *Taking Advantage of Media*, Laurie Brown describes the experiences of children who have become engaged by different media of communication. Using as a point of departure Marshall McLuhan's famous aphorism 'The medium is the message,' she systematically and sensitively reviews an intriguing literature – covering the technological span from radio to computers, and the age span from toddlers to teenagers. Her favourite vehicle for this survey is the cross-medium study, where the same, or similar, contents are presented via two different media – say, a picture book and a film – and the different responses exhibited by children illuminate a medium's particular genius as well as its peculiar limitations. This simple but powerful technique reveals much about the media, much about children, and more than a little about the adult experience as well.

Laurie Brown's survey calls into question numerous classical contrasts even as it confounds many of our standard expectations and commonly held assumptions. It is customary to contrast education and entertainment, but Laurie Brown repeatedly shows how the best materials embody both functions. Form and content are typically set in opposition but this book shows how the form of presentation in fact constitutes an important aspect of its content. Scientific research about education is often (and often appropriately) dismissed as irrelevant to daily practice but, in Laurie Brown's skilled hands, scientific studies spring to life and inform significant decisions about what children should learn and how they can best learn it. Received truths are also undermined. After reading this book, you will not be caught saying that radio is dead, that computers can only transmit technological knowledge, that young children have no aesthetic sense, that superheroes are a waste of time, or that television stifles the imagination. This is because Laurie Brown knows how to design and to describe a revealing study and to relate it to issues which have often been considered too important to be left to the research community.

Laurie Brown provides more than a cogent summary of important research, more even than a bracing challenge to our unexamined prejudices. Her most valuable gift to the reader – be you a parent, a teacher, a student, a policy maker, or indeed anyone interested in children, media, and education – is a framework for thinking about how anyone learns from 'mediated presentations.' Armed with the knowledge in this book, any reader should henceforth be able to make informed decisions about which book or television show or computer game to select, how to present these materials to children (or to oneself), how to evaluate the effectiveness of the medium and then make a shrewd guess about which media experience might serve as a suitable 'follow up.'

Laurie Brown succeeds in this daunting assignment because she is deeply immersed in her subject matter, because she has reflected upon it for many years, and because she is committed to communicating her conclusions clearly and succinctly to individuals actively involved with children. Trained in several forms, involved professionally with television, books and other media, a highly regarded scholar in educational psychology and in the science of communication, Laurie Brown is uniquely equipped to synthesize her own findings with those of other leading investigators and to introduce them to a wider community.

As a result of her pioneering research, and her capacity to work so effectively, Laurie Brown has fleshed out McLuhan's aphorism. Through numerous compelling examples we come to see how the medium in which a story is told, or a concept expressed, shapes the way in which the material is presented, apprehended, stored, interpreted, and ultimately drawn upon for various uses. We confront the possibility that even the most basic categories of experience – space, time, feelings, goals – have engraved themselves upon our consciousness by virtue of the media in which we typically encounter them. How fortunate it is that these powerful ideas have themselves been conveyed in a medium that is well-suited for this task – and especially so, when that medium is deployed by a masterful communicator.

Preface and acknowledgments

Every time a new technology becomes a storyteller, its effect on children's well-being is debated. When motion pictures became popular, parents worried that seeing movies would degrade their children's conduct and morals. In 1928, the Motion Picture Research Council invited a group of psychologists to measure the movies' effects on children. These investigators concluded in a predictably obscure little volume: 'Nothing of equal interest to children has happened in the world of drama before.' Children can learn more about adult drama from movies, they reported, than was ever possible from books or theater. Such a powerful medium deserves special handling when it comes to educating children. Sound familiar?

These days, children under twelve are increasingly occupied with tales transmitted by the media: they spend an alarming number of hours watching broadcast television and now video cassettes, attend theatrical movies with friends instead of parents, participate in computer-driven adventures not just in arcades but in their living rooms and classrooms, and visit libraries that house much more than books. Concern over media effects mounts as new technologies enter the home and school at an accelerated rate.

Every responsible adult should understand how each medium shapes a story and, in turn, a child's grasp of the message. Fiction is our society's great informal tutor; it offers children values to adopt, fantasies to wish for, heroes and heroines to model behavior after – all painlessly, without children being aware of receiving an education along with their entertainment. What does television drama teach children at different ages? Can they benefit from computers' interactive fiction? We need to know what are a medium's distinct capabilities and limitations and how they affect youngsters' developing minds. Only then can we help children take full advantage of all storytelling media.

More often than not, scholars report their insights to a select audience of peers already well versed in the subject. While this exchange of views within a professional community is necessary, it ignores the general public's right to be kept well-informed. This seems especially ill-advised in a field like mine, which studies what children learn from the media – a field whose findings speak to so many people's lives.

I have therefore written this book to share the results of my work with all those who care about children and their encounters with literature and the media.

This book is based on a six-year-long program of research comparing children's responses to stories in various media, and there are many people whose help along the way I want to acknowledge.

I am first of all grateful to the hundreds of children who gave of their time to help me understand their views of fiction and reality. Special thanks to the Watertown, Massachusetts public school students, teachers, librarians, principals, and former Art Director Frank Peros, for their sustained indulgence of my curiosity.

My second debt is to the Harvard Graduate School of Education, where I could pursue both my academic and professional interests as an educational psychologist. Without Harvard Project Zero Director Howard Gardner's invitation to join and later direct one of the project's research teams, I would not have been able to address such basic questions about the relationship between media and the developing mind. Howard Gardner's fine intellect and sensitivity to cognition and the arts made him a perfect if demanding colleague. We were fortunate as well to have an excellent research staff, whose good ideas and long hours in the field are reflected throughout this book. Thanks especially to Gail Banker, Cynthia Char, David Fernie, Leona Jaglom, Hope Kelly, Patricia Morison, Shari Robinson and Martha Vibbert. Also to my very competent and sympathetic colleagues at Project Zero, Ellen Winner and Dennie Wolf. However, it was only because of continuing financial support from the John and Mary R. Markle Foundation that we could carry out systematic studies whose findings built on one another. My gratitude to its President Lloyd Morrisett, for his generosity and confidence in our work.

I also want to acknowledge my first home at Harvard, the Center for Research in Children's Television, and its Director Gerald Lesser, who taught me that the simplest question is often the most powerful one. Thanks as well to Professors Courtney Cazden, Barbara Flagg and David

Pillemer for their enthusiastic support of my early interest in children's story learning from the media.

It was during my several years at the Center that I was able to document effects on young viewers of that potent medium message, the television commercial. For this opportunity I am grateful to the National Science Foundation, the Federal Trade Commission, Shirley Mueller, then Director of the Better Business Bureaus' Children's Advertising Review Unit, and consumer lobbyist Robert Choate. I owe special debts to my former employer Gene Reilly, who introduced me to advertisers' questions about media impact on children, and to Action for Children's Television President Peggy Charren, who inspired me to conduct research that would serve children's interests first.

Many people deserve credit for contributing to specific chapters.

Gavriel Salomon, Professor at Hebrew University, whose probing questions about the interaction of media, cognition and learning had a formative influence on my thinking, as expressed particularly in chapter 1.

Deborah Wadsworth, Program Officer at the Markle Foundation, who asked me to host task force meetings on the future of children's radio. Here I heard the well-informed viewpoints of Don Druker and Louisa Nielson from the National Endowments, producers George Morency, Joyce Hill and Pat Connor, researcher Richard Forsythe, theater director Candace Barrett, and others. I am also appreciative of New York's Museum of Broadcasting, where the history of American radio drama is available to anyone with the time to listen.

Staff of the Boston Public Library, especially Jane Manthorne, Special Projects, and Irenemarie Cullinane, Children's Literature Specialist, for inviting me to share my ideas with an international audience of children's book authors and illustrators. Also Phyllis Lindsey, Children's Librarian at the superb public library in Hingham, Massachusetts, for reading sections of chapter 3.

Laura Simms, who by her skill as a storyteller is forever reminding me of the magic that fiction offers both teller and audience.

Mort Schindel, President of Weston Woods Studios, for making available film and video story materials and sound studio facilities, as well as for his encouragement in the project's early stages.

Alfred Guzzetti, Professor at Harvard University's Carpenter Center for Visual Arts, for upgrading my love for the cinema with rigorous coursework in film editing and analysis. Filmmakers Robert Breer and Mary Beams, who taught me the painstaking but joyful craft of animation. Also the University Film and Video Study Center at MIT and the National Association of Broadcasters, both of which provided financial assistance for my filmmaking activities.

Maureen Gaffney, Director of the Media Center for Children; Ernst Emrich, Secretary of the Prix Jeunesse International; and John Murray and Gavriel Salomon, organizers of the Boys Town Conference on the Future of Children's Television, all of whom offered me opportunities to speak before various audiences and in so doing refine the views about children's television viewing and imagination reported in chapter 6.

Joseph Walters of Project Zero, David Dockterman of Tom Snyder Productions, Ross Harris of Computer Graphics in Education, Andee Rubin of Bolt, Baranek & Newman, Susan Jo Russell of Technical Education Research Center and also Donna DeBonis of Farrell, Pennsylvania public schools, Beth Lowd of Lexington, Massachusetts public schools, and Joey Stone Bear at the Santa Cruz, California public school libraries, all of whom informed my writing on computers in chapter 8.

Without the right publisher, even the best of book manuscripts will fall into oblivion. I owe a particular debt to Carol Baker, whose commitment to the book and thoughtful editorial comments persisted beyond the call of duty. My gratitude also to Robert Paul, for wanting to make academic research more accessible to the public, and to Stratford Caldecott, who graciously picked up the editorial ball in mid-course and helped me see the project through to completion.

My agent Phyllis Wender also deserves to be acknowledged many times over. I have enjoyed her help throughout the writing of this book, from proposal to promotion. Thank you, Phyllis.

I am grateful to Margaret Erickson, a highly professional and meticulous typist, whose help in the final preparation of this manuscript was a godsend.

Very special thanks to my stepsons, Tolon and Tucker, whose opinions about the television shows, movies, theater and books we have shared I always appreciate and find helpful.

Finally, I want to thank Marc Brown, whose involvement in the research at Project Zero turned into a permanent love affair. He has lived through the long preparation of this book offering me the kind of patience, good humor and support that every writer of a first book dreams of having.

Laurene Krasny Brown
Hingham, Massachusetts
February 1985

Picture credits

Grateful acknowledgment is made to the following for permission to reprint previously published material.

Figure 3.3: Gail E. Haley, from *A Story a Story*. Copyright © 1970 by Gail E. Haley. Reprinted by permission of Atheneum Publishers, Inc. and the illustrator.

Figure 3.4: Mitsumasa Anno, from *Anno's Journey*. Copyright © 1977 by Fukiunkan Shoten Publishers. Reprinted by permission of Philomel Books and the Bodley Head.

Figure 3.5: Maurice Sendak, from *Where the Wild Things Are*. Copyright © 1963 by Maurice Sendak. Reprinted by permission of Harper and Row, Publishers, Inc. and the Bodley Head.

Figure 3.6: Steven Kellogg, from *Pinkerton Behave!*. Copyright © 1979 by Steven Kellogg. Reprinted by permission of Dial Books for Young Readers/E. P. Dutton, Inc., Frederick Warne Ltd, and Sheldon Fogelman.

Figure 4.1: Ed Young, from *The Lion and the Mouse: An Aesop Fable* by Aesop. Copyright © 1979 by Ernest Benn Ltd. Reprinted by permission of Doubleday & Company, Inc. and A. and C. Black Ltd.

Figure 4.2: Ralph Pinto, from *Aesop Fables* retold by Joan Hirschmann. Copyright © 1964. Reprinted from a Harlan Quist Book reprinted by Dell Publishing Company, Inc.

Figure 4.3: Wenceslaus Hollar, from *Aesop: Five Centuries of Illustrated Fables* selected by John J. McKendry. Copyright © 1964 by the Metropolitan Museum of Art. Reprinted by permission of the Metropolitan Museum of Art. Originally appeared in 1665 edition of fables translated by Sir Roger L'Estrange.

Figure 4.5: Nardini, from *My Book of Aesop's Fables* retold by Jane Carruth. Copyright © 1962. Reprinted from a Fratelli Fabbri book distributed by Maxton Publishing, Inc.

Figure 4.6: John Rae, from *Fables in Rhyme for Little Folks* adapted from the French of La Fontaine and written by W. T. Larned. Copyright © 1918. Reprinted from a P. F. Volland Company book.

Figure 4.7: Milo Winter, from *The Aesop for Children*. Copyright © 1919 by Rand McNally & Company. Reprinted by permission of Rand McNally.

Figure 4.8: J. J. Grandville, from *Fables from Aesop* by Ennis Rees. Copyright © 1964 by Ennis Rees. Reprinted by permission of Oxford University Press. Originally appeared in 1883 edition of fables.

Figure 4.9: Alexander Calder, from *Aesop Fables*. Copyright © 1967. Reprinted by permission of Dover Publications, Inc. Originally appeared in 1931 edition of fables published by Harrison of Paris.

Figures 5.1, 5.2, 5.4, 5.5, 5.6 and 5.7: Film frames after Gail E. Haley, from *A Story a Story*. Copyright © 1973 by Weston Woods Studios, Inc. Reprinted by permission of Weston Woods Studios, Inc.

Figures 5.8, 5.9, 5.10, 5.11, 5.15, 5.16, 5.17 and 5.18: Film frames after Tomi Ungerer, from *The Three Robbers*. Copyright © 1972 by Weston Woods Studios, Inc. Reprinted by permission of Weston Woods Studios, Inc.

Figures 5.12, 5.13 and 5.14: Tomi Ungerer, from *The Three Robbers*. Copyright © 1962 by Tomi Ungerer. Reprinted by permission of Atheneum Publishers, Inc.

Figures 6.6, 6.12 and 6.18: Film frames traced from *The Fisherman and His Wife*. Copyright © 1977 by Bosustow Productions.

Figure 8.1: Computer program screen by Milton Bradley, from *Vocabulary Skills: Context Clues*. Copyright © 1982. Reprinted by permission of Media Materials, Inc.

Figure 8.2: Computer program screen by Tom Snyder Productions, from *Swiss Family Robinson*, product of Windham Classics, Inc. Copyright © 1984. Reprinted by permission of Tom Snyder Productions.

Figure 8.3: Computer program screen by Learningways, from *Master-Type's Writing Wizard*, product of Scarborough Systems. Copyright © 1984. Reprinted by permission of Learningways.

Chapter 1

Why the medium matters

It matters in what medium children experience a story. There are differences among media with profound implications for children's developing minds. But they are not the disparities most often researched and debated.

How media differ

Content   It is not a simple case of media offering different fantasy diets, although content cannot just be dismissed. Children do seek out one medium over another to experience certain material. Young American viewers turn on television Saturday mornings expecting cartoon adventures, not news. Today's teenagers rely on radio for music, not drama. Adults tend to think in terms of media content and characters too. We rate the appropriateness of movie subject matter for minors, complain about commercial television's abundant violent heroes, and bring home picture books with friendlier, fuzzier protagonists.

Important as they are, content differences among media must not be exaggerated. For one thing, the same story-line routinely crosses media boundaries. Children's books are rewritten as screenplays. Conversely, film and television characters are licensed for nonbroadcast use in books, magazines and comics, to say nothing of toys and t-shirts. Media content also evolves with changing times and technologies; screen adventurers are busier now settling outer space than the American west. At the same time, apparent differences in story settings sometimes disguise similar dramatic themes, in this instance overcoming evil in the interest of settling a new frontier.

Patterns of use Nor does the medium matter just because each format's storytelling takes place under different physical and social circumstances. To see a movie, we take children to a theater where they sit in a crowd in the dark. To watch television, children can be alone at home relaxing in bed. In both cases the intimacy is between child and screen image. In contrast, to have a storybook read aloud is automatically a shared experience between child and reader.

But patterns of media use change too. During World War Two, families sat around the piece of furniture that was a radio and listened together. Today compact Walkman radios are worn like apparel, and no one in the room but the wearer hears the message. Television viewing also is changing. When children tape programs off the air for later viewing using video cassette recorders and readily scan show material on video disc, their use of video more closely resembles the control exercised when reading a book. Now that computers and television are bedfellows, children play games on their monitors instead of watching games played on them.

Form Form is the most profound, enduring difference between media. Every medium tells a story in its own way. Each form the narrative assumes offers new information. 'All media are active metaphors in their power to translate experience into new forms.'[1] Marshall McLuhan popularized this idea in the 1960s, but without the benefit of empirical evidence.

What makes a medium's storytelling distinctive? First, every medium has a particular physical makeup of sound, pictures and print. Radio delivers a story using strictly auditory means. Audiovisual media like television and film distinguish themselves by combining sounds (speech, music and sound effects) at a fixed pace with moving images. Where paint, canvas and brushes constitute an artist's physical materials, analogous technical means for a television director include cameras, microphones, lights and actors.

Second, a medium represents story content using specific symbols like verbal language, drawn images and gestures. The same medium, radio, may use such different symbol systems as language and music, just as the same symbol system, language, may occur in different media like radio and books. Symbols differ in what they reveal about their referents. Pictures are well suited for depicting visible aspects of stories such as how characters look or where they are in a setting, whereas verbal language readily conveys nonvisible ones like what a character is thinking. Finer variations are possible within a given symbol system; a drawn image allows the artist more leeway than does a photograph to select which of an object's features to include or accentuate.

Third, each medium adopts certain rules and habits for handling its physical and symbolic resources. Although both film and television are capable of repeating shots, only television uses the instant replay to give viewers another chance to see dramatic moments in live sports broadcasts. Even within the same medium, different techniques come in and out of favor; where once a gradual dissolve out of one scene into the next was called for in a film, now a simple jump cut will do.

How media affect children's story learning

What children know of a story reflects its distinctive delivery. Children's knowledge of the Star Wars saga (its space settings, fantastic characters, struggles between good and evil forces in the galaxy) depends on whether they see the movie or hear the radio serialization. Media bias how children process a story, what information they acquire, and which styles and production techniques become familiar to them. Although these biases interact with one another, let's consider them one at a time.

Processing a story   Each story medium calls on children to do different mental work. To be grasped, a story must be decoded, read, unwrapped. Radio stories demand aural comprehension of words, sound effects and music. Printed fiction requires that children be literate with written words. Pictured stories call for facility with drawings or photographs. Television and film ask children to integrate sound and picture information. Every time children experience a story, they are practicing the mental acts necessary to extract meaning from a given medium's delivery. Practice improves performance. Children who do more leisure reading at home achieve higher reading scores at school.[2] But what mental skills does experience with nonprint media develop? Is all that TV viewing good for anything besides arguments over bedtime and breakfast?

3

This is no trivial question. The skills children cultivate deciphering a medium's fiction likely have more general use as well. Each form of experience, including time spent with the media, produces a certain intelligence for dealing with or thinking about the world.[3] It is well accepted that verbal language influences thought. Consider how readily we equate thinking with talking to ourselves, or how frustrating it is not to find the right words to express an idea. Do nonlinguistic symbols also serve as tools of thought? After all, architects and sculptors have to become adept at imagining objects in the round, illustrators at composing two-dimensional pictures. Experience with images from books, TV, and video games likewise enhances children's 'visual literacy:' their skill at reading pictures, the vividness of their mental imagery, their ability to remember picture information and produce images themselves, their sense of what is beautiful.

As but one example, consider how children learn to read transitions between camera long shots and close-ups. When psychologist Gavriel Salomon showed fifth graders a narrative film that cut from long shots directly to close-ups, he found their story comprehension varied with a more general skill, that of relating parts of a picture to the whole.[4] Without some minimal ability to relate parts to a whole, children presented this film had trouble seeing it was the same scene being shown from different distances. Another film version substituted gradual zooms in and out from long shots to close-ups. Now children's story understanding was unrelated to mastery of this skill. In Salomon's terms, watching zooms 'supplants' and also 'models' this mental act.

Children learn physical behavior they see in film and on television. Why can't they also become familiar enough with certain graphic and cinematic techniques to apply them in thinking about other situations? Experience with zooms, and relating parts to a whole, may help children assemble puzzles, make maps, and focus in on details. Such transfer effects are hard to pin down. But we may overlook important learning if we don't even consider how children process different media content.

Learning a story What children know of a story varies with the medium. The information different symbols highlight about story content is reflected in children's learning. For example, of what consequence is it for children's story comprehension that pictures are better than words at depicting visible aspects of things? What is visible about story characters includes their general appearance, costume, facial expressions, gestures and physical relationship to other characters and objects in a setting. No amount of verbal description substitutes for the dense information pictures provide. One kind of symbol never fully explains another kind of symbol. As you will see, bringing to mind images of performing characters helps children, more consistently than remembering prose descriptions, to infer their physical traits, temperament and feelings. Even preschoolers can interpret the feelings on a character's face, although they use a limited vocabulary to report those emotions. Listening to actors and actresses speak informs children about characters' age, nationality and mood in ways that reading their dialogue does not.

Only when a medium tells a story in a fashion respectful of its production means, however, should we expect medium differences in learning. Television producers may choose an eventful drama over one filled with introspective monologues. Then they can take advantage of the many camera and editing techniques that move characters through space. Use of medium-specific techniques varies from production to production. In the early days of instructional television, directors sat a teacher before a stationary camera and filmed the lesson. No wonder there were no significant learning differences when TV and live classroom teaching were compared.[5]

Medium differences in what children learn from stories matter in the long run as well as right now. This book pays special attention to how children's first experience of a story is shaped by the format, be it radio, book, television or computer. But over time children accumulate experience with whatever story content a medium consistently stresses. They have so many opportunities to attend to, remember, interpret, perhaps even prefer this content to other sorts of information.

One useful way to tap learning differences due to the medium is by comparing what children know of the same story presented in alternative formats. Much of the evidence I will review was obtained by making such comparisons. Every time one medium version of a story is contrasted to another, certain properties of each stand out. Pit film against TV and questions come to mind about image size and scale. Compare picture books with television and the shift from still to moving pictures is highlighted. Contrast radio with television and now the picture content emerges as a whole. Knowing how media differ as sources of story content helps us predict children's responses to each format. Moreover, much of what children learn from a story is accessible to interested adults. Exploring what children notice, remember, infer, imagine, and feel about a story is revealing, especially when you know what to look and listen for.

Appreciating story expression Children's aesthetic – their savoring of

5

production techniques, artistic styles, and all the expressive means a story uses – is influenced by their exposure to fiction in different media. Young audiences' familiarity with specific narrative styles and treatments breeds preferences for the way they want different stories to look and sound. Experience with television and computer graphics extends children's art education into the fields of commercial art and electronic technology.

Young children appreciate a story's means of production intuitively. Preschoolers hearing a recorded story readily pick out rhyming words, melodies and sound effects to rehearse. Children watching television spontaneously imitate characters' idiosyncrasies. This is a natural, appropriate way to enjoy a story. Verse, music and sound effects are there to add information and ambience without distracting listeners away from the plot. Actors practice their characters' mannerisms to make them appear 'in character.' These expressive features are effective because of their transparency.

It is premature to speak of young children's tacit experience of style as aesthetic appreciation. There is not the necessary emotional and intellectual detachment. Nor are young audiences usually aware of formal features apart from content. Without specific training, younger children tend to describe and group paintings in terms of *what* they depict, not *how*. Researchers find that interest in painting style *per se* is not expressed until children are in the upper elementary grades.[6] By that age, children also can step outside their involvement with a story to figure out a special effect or criticize an unrealistic portrayal. Yet younger children are no less opinionated than older ones about the illustration styles they like or dislike. As you will see, their choice of picture book is often based on its looks. Sensitivity to form is no less important when it occurs without valuing a work as an artistic product. It is where taste begins.

Stories children grow up with influence their adult appreciation of fiction. What adult audiences call good animation may depend on whether they grew up with Walt Disney or Hanna-Barbera. Influence also filters down. We introduce children to fiction that stands out from our childhood memories, and they will do the same. This makes for classics and gives culture continuity.

Out of every adult population emerges the next generation of storytellers. It is no coincidence that a new technology at first adopts the expressive habits of its predecessor. Film recreated theater. Television illustrated radio. This happens whenever the people responsible for creating stories in one medium were raised on another. Over time, a popular medium's storytelling style seeps into children's ways of expressing themselves. Children growing up today will bring to the storytelling media of the twenty-first century television images they watch after school this afternoon.

Why media matter more for children

The choice of story medium matters more for children than for adults. This is not to belittle adult sensitivity. What changes with age is only the form our responsiveness to media assumes. Yet certain of children's immaturities make them especially vulnerable to fiction and its varied formats.

What makes children special as a story audience? I single out three reasons: believing in magic, judging a book by its cover, and never having been to the moon.

Believing in magic, fairies, and superheroes Young children (below age eight) experience a story as having reality far beyond that attributed it by adults. Not that young children don't know a story when they hear one. Quite the contrary. Very young children can tell a story apart from other uses of language. Arthur Applebee analyzed a large collection of stories invented by children and found storytellers as young as two years old using such narrative conventions as formal openings ('Once upon a time'), consistent past tense, and formal closings ('happily ever after' or 'The end').[7] But it easily eludes a kindergartener that what happens in a story is hypothetical. The difference between fantasy and reality is not so clear or stable. Even some six-year-olds will defend the reality of a fairy tale, explaining: 'Cinderella is a real person, she just lives far away,' or 'Little Red Riding Hood really happened, but a long time ago.'

Of course, children are getting more and more sophisticated. Word gets out early: the blood is only ketchup, Superman uses wires. But even when young children admit a story is pretend, even when they can proudly recite all the physical impossibilities they use as clues – 'People can't fly unless they take an airplane,' 'There's no such thing as talking animals' – that pretense still creeps into a child's sense of reality, especially when he or she is alone in bed at night. Young children are more forgetful of the boundary between their reality and that of the story. No matter how sophisticated, they readily enter invented worlds and accept their ground rules.

It also slips by younger audiences that fiction is a figment of someone's imagination. Stories stand more on their own. Miraculously, they spring whole into the world. Most young people only vaguely connect stories with the real people responsible for them, unless they have direct contact with those people: they do not consider what an author is trying to say or how well an actress performs her role. When the movie credits roll down the screen, there's still time to ask for popcorn. That lack of awareness adds further to a story's reality and to young children's intense experience of fiction.

Judging a book by its cover   Young children's thinking relies heavily on perception. Between roughly ages four and seven, children go through a stage where the perceptible, as opposed to more abstract, attributes of things shape their model of reality.[8] Older children's and adults' thought also is influenced by their perception; the difference is one of degree. Young children group objects together because they look alike, not because they do similar work or share some other less visible criterion. They will find only one aspect of an object salient and ignore others. They cannot imagine as readily as older children that a situation looks different from other people's viewpoints.

As one consequence, young audiences rely more on what they see to tell apart reality and fantasy. In two studies conducted at Harvard, children ages seven, nine and twelve picked which one of a pair of print materials or TV shows they thought was more real and said why.[9] ('Why?' and 'How do you know?' are two of the most revealing questions to hear children answer.) For the youngest children, form overrides content.

Evaluating the reality status of print, they make frequent reference to books' physical features. They say a hardcover book is more real than its paperback edition, and a fanciful story that has photographs (*The Red Balloon*) is more real than a believable story with drawn illustration (*Homer Price*). The more realistic the pictures, the 'realer' the book.

Young children also pay more attention to television's surface features. By age seven they may explain how Superman isn't real: 'It's only trick cameras. When he bends things and crashes rocks with his hands and flies, that's all tricks. He's just holded up with giant ropes that have invisible glue.' But when choosing which is more real, live-action Superman or animated Charlie Brown, the answer is invariably Superman, because 'Charlie Brown is only a cartoon.' No matter how plausible a character is Charlie Brown. No matter how impossible is Superman's behavior. Young viewers are more convinced by whichever drama looks more real.

Of the two media, assessing television fiction presents the greater challenge. Young children say more often and from an earlier age that books are written by someone and aren't necessarily true. This recognition seems more elusive with television. Why the difference? There are several reasons. Seeing one or two names paired with a book title seems to mean more to children than the quickly presented credits acknowledging collective responsibility for a television program. Writing their own stories also helps children understand the idea of book authorship. Having no experience producing television keeps that process remote and mysterious. This may change the more that children tape shows on video cassette recorders and create video images with computers. Most of all, young children cannot easily dismiss the illusion of reality that television so effectively achieves. Television appears to present the world as it is, whereas print and illustration are more blatantly symbols. Lights, microphones, cue cards, special effects, all remain off-camera. The seams in good editing go unnoticed. All these production means are out of sight, and for young children that suggests out of mind.

Yet younger children read pictures with more skill than they read words. They understand stories better when they are illustrated.[10] They rely more on pictures than sound to make sense of a TV or movie drama.[11] As you will discover, introducing young children to stories in a highly visual medium like television gives them a certain edge in learning fiction. The same lifelike appearance that makes photographs so convincing also makes them readily meaningful to young audiences. Drawn illustrations, if less believable, are no less accessible. The difficult question is whether fostering skill with pictures comes at the expense of developing language and other conceptual skills. Because young children's tools of thought are not fully formed, whether we cultivate some mental skills and neglect others makes a critical difference.

Never having been to the moon   More of what young children encounter in fiction is new to them. Novelty is a function of what an audience already knows, and children have a lower threshold than adults for the unfamiliar.

Two things happen every time children experience fiction. One is, children try to understand a story in terms of what they already know; they 'assimilate' a story into their existing ideas and beliefs. At the same time, what they already know is changed (clarified, elaborated, even contradicted) by incoming information. When youngsters' existing knowledge is inadequate to comprehend a story, they may 'accommodate' and learn something new.

Fiction helps shape children's basic ideas about subjects with which they have little direct experience. Many American children know more from TV dramas about committing crimes, enforcing the law, being in hospital and being in the army than they do from firsthand experience. Almost all of us know from the media what it's like to walk on the moon. Were the whole event staged in a television studio, how would we know? Perhaps one reason young audiences so enjoy characters who exist only in fiction, who have no real-life counterpart – like ghosts, dragons, fairies, and smurfs – is because there is no competing real-world information to confuse matters. Children can know a fantastic universe intimately. Along similar lines, young children may ask to hear the same story again and again partly because they can predict so successfully what happens next. For young audiences, knowledge of the real world is informed by fantasy, and fantasy is more real.

Young children are also learning what to expect from literature and the media. The foods we feed children define their early eating habits. Like diet, the stories we serve children determine what they call legitimate and likable fiction. Children learn not only what kinds of fantasies each medium offers, but also how different stories look and sound. If it's an action adventure, expect a fast-moving hero. If it's a situation comedy, expect a laugh track. The narrower a medium's fictional range, the more well-defined and restricted will be children's standards. The more varied a medium's fiction, the wider children's appetite. The specific options a medium exercises to tell its stories at a given time are only a small sample of what it can do. Young audiences cannot know what they are missing.

The case of older children Development is such a gradual process, and children differ so much among themselves, that descriptions of stages in children's thinking are more like pencil sketches than finished art. Still, they give an impression of how audiences of different ages approach fiction.

Older children (roughly between ages eight and twelve) draw firmer lines between reality and fantasy. Like adults, they are more aware of suspending disbelief to participate in a story. Older audiences appreciate subtler grades of fiction; an historical drama based on facts is partly true. A story loses credibility for them if an actor's performance is too exaggerated or the plot too unlikely. For example, consider sixth graders' comments about *Little House on the Prairie*, a TV family drama set during the Depression. The show isn't real, explains one twelve-year-old, because 'each week they have a new problem, but in true life you really don't ever have so many problems as they have, even if you're poor.'[12]

Or from a more pessimistic child: 'They'll be just playing and all of a sudden they get these problems . . . and then suddenly something good happens and it always turns out all perfect and fine. That's not real.' Whether they focus on too many problems or too easy solutions, these children are reasoning at a higher level about the reality status of fiction. They are not asking whether a story-line is possible or impossible, but rather how plausible an account it is.

Older children understand better that fiction is invented. They can step outside their involvement with a story to criticize it or offer praise. No longer as seduced by the magic of fantasy, older story consumers are interested in knowing how stories are made. They appreciate the rules governing story logic, they want to crack the production codes. Analytic skills are reinforced in school where children this age practice finding the important information in prose, learn to support their opinions with evidence, and prepare book reports. Older boys and girls still harbor fierce, though fickle, loyalties to fictional characters; the difference is that now they are equally curious about authors, directors, actors and actresses.

With age also comes greater facility with language. The more children can think in words, the less tied they are to immediate experience. Children learn to overlook apparent changes in things and recognize their constant features; the same quantity of water poured into different shaped glasses yields the same amount to drink. Older audiences are better equipped than younger ones to pick out common content from various story versions. More abstract thinking protects their sense of story from changes in illustration style, production values and casting. Older girls and boys can read below a story's surface, where meaning across different adaptations remains more stable.

Yet the story medium matters for older children too. As children gain competence with symbols, they extract more information from media, including the content each medium emphasizes. As you will see, older children interpreting a story draw more fully on the cues each medium provides. Rather than simply noticing what a TV character is doing, as young viewers are apt to do, older viewers will derive a character's personality from studying his or her behavior: 'Fonz is cool,' 'Joanie won't do things she's not supposed to except for a very important reason' (characters from the show *Happy Days*). More of what any medium's fiction has to offer is available to an older audience. They follow more complex plots,[13] account better for characters' feelings and motives,[14] and reflect about a story's moral or theme.

With every passing day, children accumulate experience of both reality and invented worlds. As they get older, children learn what to expect from different stories. Older viewers know exactly when to stop fooling around with a younger brother or sister and return their attention to the screen. By listening to the soundtrack, they can predict when something important in a drama is about to occur. They also can tell when a story is missing basic content. When two of my colleagues read children a fairy tale with the characters' motives omitted, older listeners, more so than younger ones, simply added motives to their own accounts of the story.[15] Based on their experience with fiction, children build up ideas about what a fairy tale or an action adventure show should be like. As a result, older audiences will be more aware of changes in a medium's storytelling habits.

Full appreciation of fiction requires attending to both the means of presentation and the meaning they convey. Interestingly, such a mature response seems to combine younger children's natural sensitivity to form and older youngster's grasp of a story's deeper message. Savoring of style and other expressive means no longer is implicit; with adequate maturity, experience and training, audience members deliberately notice how well a medium is being used to narrate.

Learning goes on in every phase of human development, at every level of intelligence and experience. That is one reason why, as Bruno Bettelheim has stressed, the same story can have different meaning for each person and even for the same person at various moments in his or her life.[16] Based on the preceding argument, certain patterns should be discernible in the ways different stories teach children. If we concur at the outset that fiction and media play significant roles in children's development, then we need to become well-informed about children's story learning from different media. Knowing how every story-bearing format communicates with children is essential; only then can we help them make the most of their experience with fiction.

Providing that information is the purpose of this book.

Hands on

We tell each other stories all the time: 'When I was your age . . .' or 'Mom, guess what happened today at school!' We often relate stories without being conscious of our role as narrator and hero, so natural, perhaps inevitable, is the impulse to narrate.

What a story needs

story: an account of an incident or series of events; a tale of any length ... of actual or fictitious events; facts or experiences that deserve narration.[17]

Stories have structure and direction; they begin, progress, and end. Stated broadly, the course of events or plot consists of somebody doing something. Stories are usually visited by some conflict or complication that needs to be resolved. In fictional stories, the problems are invented: the princess desires a husband but is forbidden to marry; the inept detective must solve a mysterious murder. Besides their sequential organization, stories have form as a whole. A story has a main idea to which all the events are relevant.

Typical stories include the following elements:[18]

a *setting*, which introduces the characters and the time and place in the story;

an *initiating event*, which leads the main character to form his or her goal and starts the sequence of events;

the *goal* or *motive*, which is the major desire of the main character;

a number of *attempts*, which are the actions of the characters;

a series of *outcomes*, which are events or states produced by the character's actions;

internal responses, which are the subgoals, thoughts, and feelings of a character leading to his or her actions;

reactions, which are thoughts or feelings produced by the outcomes of actions; and

the *resolution* or final consequence of the story.

In the following short story, based on an Aesop fable, each statement has been labeled as a story component.

'The Dog and His Shadow'

setting	(1)	Once there was a big brown dog named Sam.
initiating event	(2)	One day, Sam found a piece of meat and was carrying it home in his mouth to eat.
internal response	(3)	Now on his way home, he had to cross a plank lying across a running brook.
attempt	(4)	As he crossed the brook,
outcome	(5)	he looked down
outcome	(6)	and saw his own shadow reflected in the water beneath.
reaction	(7)	He thought it was another dog with another piece of meat.
goal	(8)	and he made up his mind to have that piece also.

attempt	(9)	So he made a snap at the shadow,
attempt	(10)	but as he opened his mouth
outcome	(11)	the piece of meat fell out.
outcome	(12)	The meat dropped into the water,
outcome	(13)	and floated away.
resolution	(14)	Sam never saw the meat again.

Making up stories with children

(1) Here is a simple way to invent stories with children.

- Think up a character for the hero or heroine.
- Place him, her, or it in a setting.
- Decide what the character wants. He might lack or seek something or have some other problem to solve.
- Take turns making up things that happen next. What does the character do to try and get what she or he wants? What problems does the hero or heroine encounter?
- Figure out a way for the main character to finally achieve his goal. Then ask: Is the story over? Has it reached a satisfying conclusion?
- Think up special endings, like: 'Snip, snap, snout, this tale's told out.'
- Try making up stories that: are funny, have sad endings, are mysterious, rhyme or repeat words, take place in outer space, happen at home, are about members of the family including pets.
- Invent a next adventure for a familiar character. Try doing this after watching a favorite TV show or reading a favorite book.
- Tape record children's story inventions for later listening. Use as gifts for relatives and friends.

(2) 'Telephone-Plus' game (any number can play)

- Sit in a circle.
- Start off a story.
- The next person repeats what you say and adds more.
- Everyone should take at least one turn in a large group (eight or more) and at least two turns in smaller groups.
- See if the person who starts the story can also complete it to the group's satisfaction.

- Rotate starters.

(3) 'What's Missing?' game (play with older children)
- Select a short story from an anthology of fables, folk-tales, or other stories.
- Read aloud, omitting one important part, such as how the story starts or what happens at the end.
- Have children guess what's been left out. Omit more and more subtle elements each time you play.

(4) 'Fairy Tale Madlib'
Have children fill in the missing words. Then read aloud the resulting story. Notice that the words supplied for (1) the hero, (2) the villain, and (3) the hero's goal are repeated in the indicated places. Invent other story frames.

Once upon a time in _____ there lived a 1_____.
               place name   adj. noun

1_____ had a _____, a _____, and a
                    noun   noun

_____. But more than anything in the world,
adj. noun

1_____ wanted to be 3_____. Alas, this goal
                        adjective

seemed impossible because 1_____ suffered under a

2_____'s evil spell. One morning, while reading a
  noun

_____ recipe book, 1_____ found a way to break
noun

the evil spell. First 1_____ mixed together _____,
                                    pl. noun

_____, and _____. Next 1_____ cooked
pl. noun   pl. noun

them, _____ all the time, until they looked like a
      verb

_____, smelled like _____, and went _____!
adj. noun   pl. noun   sound

When the steaming brew was done, 1_____ invited the

2_____ for a very _____ snack. Sure enough, the
adjective

_____ **2**_____ accepted. But after eating,
adjective

2_____ felt a little bit _____. 'What's in this snack,
adjective

anyway?' gasped the **2**_____. 'I will reveal the

ingredients if you break my evil spell,' replied the

1_____. 'That's not fair!' argued the **2**_____. But

now **2**_____ was also feeling _____. So it was
adjective

agreed. And that is how **1**_____ outsmarted the

2_____ and became **3**_____.

Chapter 2

Should children still listen?

Can you imagine your family settling down in the evening and tuning in a favorite drama on the radio console? After all, not so very long ago radio was a primary source of stories for both children and adults. Youngsters in the 1940s looked forward to *hearing* the latest episode of such shows as *The Lone Ranger*, *The Shadow* and *Our Miss Brooks*. What happened?

These days when the family settles down in the evening, some form of video most likely furnishes the fantasies. Children in the 1980s anticipate *seeing* their favorite shows on television, cable, or on video cassette.

Not that radio has disappeared from our lives. Far from it. There are more radios in America today than televisions and telephones combined.[1] Count the radios in your house. But radio listening has changed. Physically, radios are smaller, more portable, and specially equipped for solo listening. Mysteriously wired pedestrians, bicyclists and bus passengers move to rhythms only they and their Walkman can hear. Radio now offers different program content too. Even with dramatic productions from *Children's Radio Theater*, *The Web*, *New Waves* and others, there is little fiction for children available on the air.

Children listening today can find music, not melodrama. But music listening presents fewer demands than listening to drama or prose. Music purists may disapprove, but most people use radio music as a backdrop for accomplishing other things.

Should there be radio fiction for children? Perhaps its scarcity speaks the truth all too loudly; if radio stories were appealing or important enough, they would persist. Why would youngsters with ready access to illustrated tales choose strictly aural ones? With television setting children's standards for fiction, pictures must seem missing more by accident than design. Telling stories on radio may also seem old-fashioned to the young. Commercial radio broadcasters voice skepticism about the economic viability of programming for children in general.[2] Audience rating services ignore the under-twelve listener.

But maybe the radio broadcasters' doubts are unwarranted. According to one knowledgeable source, 'There's every indication from parents and kids that there's a real audience for children's radio. But we've [not] given it a real chance. You need a block of good programs . . . and lots of money for promotion.'[3] Today's compact radios and earphones allow for such intimate listening. Whether amid a crowded street or under the covers in bed, modern radio and audio cassettes might set a wonderful stage for the most personal storytelling – where children's own visions of the world can prevail.

This chapter examines the educational evidence for and against having children within earshot of audio fiction. Are children losing out on a learning experience by not listening any more?

What children miss, listening

'Listen and attend,' invites a story record narrator in her friendliest voice. But make no mistake about it: that means work. A young listener must keep up with the passing flow of words, yet has no control over their speed. And even when listening to an ideal rate of speech, sustaining attention to an unseen voice takes concentration. What is there to look at? What are your hands supposed to do? Young listeners also must make sense of what they hear and reconstruct a meaningful message in their own mind. No wonder listening to recorded prose leaves so many young children restless and bored, or asleep. Youngsters who grew up with radio must have faced the same problems; yet its stories managed to capture their attention and loyalty.

The demands of story listening take their toll. Researchers comparing different versions of the same story find children neither remember nor understand radio fiction as well as they do that in illustrated books[4] or on television.[5] Young listeners include more wrong information retelling a radio story and answer fewer factual questions correctly. Note, however, that what these investigators call 'radio' is often just a recorded reading of a story, rather than a full dramatization.

Having to rely on words alone limits children's story understanding. With no additional cues from pictures, sound effects, or music, children may be unable to decipher new words or complex sentences. Admittedly, hearing words in context does offer clues to their meaning. To astute young listeners, the sentence: 'Then [Ananse] filled the doll's bowl with pounded yams'[6] may suggest yams are something to eat. But this clue is available in other media versions as well. Hearing words with expression also may help explain them. In the 'yams' case, however, even trying to make them sound delicious in no way reveals their identity. The more key words and phrases children miss, listening, the less their grasp of and interest in the text.

Oral stories also present problems when children reason beyond the given text. To understand a story in any medium requires making all kinds of inferences, from the grammatical (to which character a pronoun refers) to the logical (what action causes what effect). A well-organized story presents information where it is needed, but it is still up to the individual to infer how these words and actions are related. Only then is a narrative coherent. Such reasoning begins right from the opening lines, as in this example from a Grimms' fairy tale, *The Fisherman and His Wife*:[7]

> There was once a poor fisherman who lived with his wife in a tiny
> hut by the sea. Each morning he went down to the shore and cast his
> net for fish. One day he pulled up a fish with gold and silver scales.

Having the first two sentences in mind, we readily deduce in the third who pulled up the fish, how, when, and where. Young children make relatively easy connections like this too. But the farther apart two story events, the more difficult it becomes for children to relate them, such as connecting a character's motive with the behavior it causes.[8]

Radio calls on audiences to contribute more inferences. Listeners do more work filling in between the lines than most other story audiences.

Even the simple reasoning above is eliminated for young TV viewers, who actually see the fisherman retrieve the fish on screen. The television picture delivers story evidence which otherwise must be inferred.

More spare story media like radio also leave fewer clues on which to base inferences. Not always is the relevant information right there in the text, as in the preceding example. This becomes especially evident when children use inferences to elaborate their knowledge of story characters, actions and settings. What kind of guy is this fisherman, anyway?

Young listeners import more outside information than viewers to answer this kind of question.[9] Visualizing the fisherman, radio listeners know at this point only that he is poor. At least that helps some nine- and ten-year-olds with costuming; they proceed to picture him in patches and ragged clothes. But there are so many details of physical appearance to account for. How old is he, for instance? Young viewers can refer to such telltale signs of age as hair color, whiskers and wrinkles. Without pictures, specific voice cues, or text, young listeners seek evidence elsewhere: they bring to bear personal experience ('He's old, because my grandpa fishes and he's old') and world knowledge, such as it is ('He's old, because fishermen are old'). But children's experience is limited, and it sometimes leads them to draw idiosyncratic or stereotyped conclusions from their listening. Thus we find errors in children's comprehension of radio stories.

Bottom-line story listening

What young listeners *do* remember from oral stories, demanding though they may be, reflects an uncanny sense of narrative form. Children retelling an oral story, one short and simple enough to be within their grasp, intuitively include the most important information and omit many minor details.[10] First graders typically mention at least one main character, an event that initiates the story, and the consequence that finally results.[11] Other content, such as characters' reactions and attempts to reach a goal, gets added as the audience matures.

Here is what one seven-year-old boy told me, recapitulating the African folktale *A Story a Story* about the origin of stories on earth:[12]

The guy wanted to have the stories.	(setting, goal)
And then the king in the sky said he	(initiating
has to pay and get all like a tiger	event)

and bees and a fairy that-no-man-has-
seen.
So he got 'em. Then he spinned a   (outcome)
web and brought them back to the king   (outcome)
of the sky.
Then he got all the stories and   (resolution)
brought them back to his village.

This is bottom-line story recall. With great economy of means, he volunteered just enough information to recreate the bare bones of the story.

Where do children get their narrative savvy? For one thing, stories identify themselves by conforming to a certain structure or plan: a text needs a setting, beginning, development and resolution to qualify as a story. Children construct an analogous mental map of story structure based on their exposure to literature. They come to expect fictional events to proceed in a prescribed manner as well – the hero will succeed in his mission, the villain will ultimately fail. The younger children are, the stronger their preference for stories organized that way.[13]

Children also learn about fiction from firsthand experience. Cause and effect relationships, essential to fiction, are tested all the time in real life; if I misbehave and pull my sister's hair (cause), will I be caught and punished (effect)? Children use what they understand about the world to evaluate the credibility of story characters, settings and events.

Young listeners' mental schemes for narratives help them organize a story as they hear it. The more a story conforms to this ideal or at least expected form, the better children remember it. When elementary school students hear a story out of order, they tend in their own accounts to reorganize events in standard sequence.[14] Children will try and make narrative sense out of scrambled picture sequences too.[15] Children's as well as adults' memory for stories simply gravitates toward the course of events to which they are accustomed.[16]

Robust as young children's basic story scheme is, it is something they don't consciously apply. Second graders perform poorly, at any rate, when asked to sort out story content in terms of its relative importance.[17] Later, when children are formally taught the rigors of story form, they discover what, in a nascent sense, they already know.

The sound of language

The memorability of oral stories does not depend solely on reliable structure or even on meaningful content. Another secret of oral literature's longevity, the one most germane to radio, is the way that it sounds in our ears. Traditional storytellers, film, television and theater, have in common with radio the power to impart sonic beauty to their verbal message. But sound matters more to radio than to any audiovisual medium. Most ephemeral of all, radio storytellers cannot speak to their audience in person or be seen in the flesh; only the relayed sound of their voices can be heard.

Spoken stories exploit the sound of language several ways. Among the most basic phonetic features oral literature employs is repetition.[18] Alliteration, rhyme and refrain all depend on sound repetition for their effect, whether at the level of letter, word or phrase. Meter and rhythm are based on repeated patterns of sound and syntax. 'It is raining' merely delivers weather information, whereas 'It is raining, raining, raining' is a more emphatic, rhythmic and expressive message. Preference also may be given to words whose sounds suggest their meaning: 'callous' characterizes a hardened person better than the softer sounding 'insensitive.' Onomatopoeic words resemble even more closely the sound of their referents – try 'splash,' 'bang,' or the more delicate 'plop.' Appropriate use of language's sensuous qualities elevates a story text from the prosaic to the poetic.

Children tend to remember poetic language in stories they hear. The very words and phrases that use sound to advantage – despite their marginal importance to the plot – appear often in young listeners' accounts.[19]

The sound of story language has greater impact on children when it is not competing with moving pictures. Radio narration elicits better recall of poetic or flavorful vocabulary than does a cartoon version of the same text; compared to viewers, school age listeners correctly identify more of a story's onomatopoeic sounds (shouts of 'eee eee'), repeated words ('It is raining, raining, raining'), and elaborative phrases (the fairy 'whom-men-never-see').[20] Listeners more often refer to characters by their formal names, 'Ananse the spider man,' whereas viewers make vague references to 'the man' or just 'him.' Even preschoolers, notorious for their brief story descriptions, include more specific wording after a strictly auditory delivery; listeners report: 'The whale ate every fish in the sea,' whereas viewers simply say, 'He ate all the fish.'[21] Once children see stories on television or film, as I later discuss, pictures become more important than words.

How aware children are of a story's use of words is debatable, however. On one hand, research indicates children pay more attention to *what* happens in a story than *how* it is told. Preschoolers will complete in identical fashion stories of similar content but opposing moods: whether the protagonist was thrown overboard in a storm or jumped overboard for a swim in the sun, he is invariably returned to his boat and sent home to bed.[22] Elementary school children asked to pick a consistent continuation for a story or poem will base their choices more on verbal content than on style.[23] After hearing this opening passage:

> How pleasant to know Mr Peer!
> Who has written such volumes of stuff!
> Some think him ill-tempered and queer,
> But a few think him pleasant enough

more students follow up with a verse further describing Mr Peer (a) than one using a consistent rhyme pattern (b).

(a) Here's a man who's very nice indeed,
   I'd like to have a book of his to read.
   Sometimes, it's true, he starts to lose his temper.
   Yet Mr Peer is pleasant each November.
(b) She sits in a beautiful parlour,
   With hundreds of tiles on the wall;
   She drinks a great deal of Marsala,
   But never gets tipsy at all.

On the other hand, children's language sensitivity may not be tapped by such rigorous tasks. For instance, young listeners will sometimes continue a story with phrases they like the sound of, regardless of whether they agree in style with the previous text. Perhaps their sense of story language, like that of its structure, is only intuitive. In that case, young listeners reveal their appreciation of poetic language by repeating its rhymes and refrains, and by asking to hear again stories that use such vocabulary.

Listening to radio drama

Listening involves attending to so much more than language. Yet we routinely equate listening comprehension with knowledge of word meanings and take for granted the significance to children of sounds – shrieks, screeches, crashes, creakings, weeping, whispers, roars, rustlings, tweets, tinkles, slaps and sighs. Only in music class are children credited with having an ear for more than semantics. Radio drama takes advantage of sound quality in several ways, the most basic of which is having each character speak his or her own part.

Voice The mental image we conjure up listening to a radio voice can be so vivid that actually seeing the person behind the microphone is surprising or downright disappointing. An actor's tone of voice lends shades of meaning typically lost in print. It helps establish a character's sex, age, mood, even physical stature. Speech accent and dialect suggest social class and nationality. A radio character's voice carries critical dramatic weight; a speaker silent too long is forgotten.

Children rely on the way people's voices sound to interpret an audio drama. Elementary school students will use characters' accents to establish the setting for a radio episode: 'I think the story [*Treasure Island*] happened in England because of the way they talk.'[24] Accent, more than any other clue, helped them correctly infer this drama's location. Nine- and ten-year-olds will base a hero's size on his voice: 'I think he's small,' ventured one boy, 'because of the way he talks – he has a small voice.'[25] I have even heard fifth graders determine a character's physical state from his breathing: 'Owl was tired of flying, he was taking deep deep breaths.'[26] Children's attention to voice is scattered throughout my media research at Harvard. This is suggestive evidence, however.

But the impact voices have on children is also common knowledge. Infants respond differently to angry shouts than to soothing whispers before they know what the respective words mean: to which remark will an infant react more cheerfully, 'I love you' spoken in a loud gruff voice or 'I hate you' said in a soft caressing tone? Toddlers comply less often to a command delivered as a thin, hesitant plea. Without dramatic coaching, adults adjust their voices to make certain impressions on children. Among radio actors, achieving such effects is a profession.

Sound effects Cockadoodledoo! A single sound can bring an entire scene to mind if it is charged with unmistakable associations.[27] Sound effects are an integral part of radio drama production. One producer explains:[28]

'Door closes' looks simple enough on the page. But how is the door to be closed? Is the character striding out of the room in a fury? If so the door needs to be banged. Or is he creeping out? If so it must be closed quietly and carefully. And how soon after the line should we hear the door? Points like this go to the heart of a play's credibility.

A radio producer's careful handling of sound is not lost on children. In one Harvard study, children ages eight through twelve identified sound effects compiled on audiotape.[29] Many subtle sound qualities emerged in their descriptions. Hearing a door open and close, then footsteps growing fainter, one third grader said: 'Someone's slamming a door and walking away inside a hall.' Notice her attention to how the door was closed (slamming), to the pace and direction of footsteps (walking away), even to the acoustical background (inside a hall).

Children associate sound effects with characters' actions, props and surroundings. Listening to the radio episode of *Treasure Island*, youngsters inferred a wintry scene 'because you could hear the wind blow,' knew the captain was in a crowded tavern 'because of the glasses and people talking in the background,' and that he paid for his drink in coins 'because you could hear them clinking.' Sound effects provide children with aural images of story content; omitting them is like removing a radio story's illustration.

Children this age also can judge whether a given sound belongs in a story. They sorted out among the sound effects on tape which ones were plausible and which inappropriate to include in this *Treasure Island* broadcast: yes, horse hoofbeats belonged; no, car traffic did not.[30]

The younger children are likely, and the more limited their vocabulary the more likely they are, to depend on sounds to follow an aural narrative – with one obvious but critical caveat. Younger children's repertoire of familiar sounds is more limited as well. Sound effects must be within listeners' experience to be effective. A child must have heard a sound before and be able to recognize it without seeing its source; for example, the identity of an old wheelbarrow rattling down the road went undetected among this youthful urban audience. Interpreting a busy soundtrack is like an informative mystery game, providing the clues are meaningful to the players listening.

Music Even babies respond to the moods music evokes. The calming effect on infants of softly sung lullabies is familiar to parents worldwide. Six-month-olds can recognize simple melodies and rhythms.[31] By age eight or nine, children have the musical ability of untrained adults.

No wonder, then, that eight- to twelve-year-olds interpreted music in the *Treasure Island* broadcast with such sensitive ears.[32] Most children described as happy an upbeat sea chanty, for example, whereas an eerie synthesizer passage sounded spooky and scary. No one confused the two effects. Music offered older children clues to story setting as well; a sailor song at one point suggested pilgrims, England, and the sea. Listeners discounted the non-Western sound of a percussive African rhythm as unsuitable for this story.

What makes music so expressive for children? First there is the distinctive way a piece of music sounds. Music is composed of several elements: pitch, melody, modality, rhythm, harmony, dynamics, tempo and timbre (a trumpet's brassiness, an oboe's reedy breath). Each musical element contributes to the overall emotional tone. According to adult judges, speeding up a piece makes it more exciting or gay; slowing it down can sadden, dignify, or calm its mood.[33] Children perceive these differences too. Some tunes just sound more cheerful to them than others.

Children also acquire emotional responses to music. *Treasure Island's* music reminded many children of past experiences with similar-sounding music: the sea chanty was reminiscent of carnivals and circuses, the synthesizer of ghost stories and horror movies.[34] As children get older, their musical associations grow more plentiful, their ears more attuned to our culture's popular musical genres and harmonies. With a flick of the radio dial most American teenagers can tell where their music loyalties lie. Audio productions can make good use of music young listeners already know and enjoy; the right opening tune can entice them into radio drama before any action takes place.

Finally, music heard in the context of radio drama has the story itself working in its favor. Although usually lacking its own subject matter, music can be composed or selected to do particular narrative work, such as defining a character or mimicking his movement. Which instrument sounds more like a fat person's footsteps, a tuba or a flute? Think of Prokofiev's *Peter and the Wolf*. The specific settings, characters and actions a story supplies must help children appreciate the flavor of accompanying music, just as music informs the accompanying verbal message.

The detection dilemma   Medium effects on children's story learning often elude our notice. Young listeners' responsiveness to sounds is a perfect example.

The problem rests in part with audience perception. Background music, especially when continuous, often influences listeners' feelings or ideas about a story without their realizing it.[35] This lack of awareness is frequently the desired outcome. Music, sounds effects, acoustic background, even intervals of silence, are expected to contribute unobtrusively to a radio drama's overall impact. The effects of such auditory features are even more subtle for young children, who know little about their production.

Nor are children trained to base story inferences on nonverbal sound clues. I have rarely heard children mention music retelling a story, even when they know its songs by heart. Sound-inclusive story listening and reporting are not encouraged or even considered in most homes and schools, where only the verbal message counts.

What children know about a story from its sounds is like a well-kept secret in which children use listening skills they may not know they possess. Gathering information from sound effects, voice and music enhances story listening so much, it deserves to be acknowledged and cultivated. Asking more direct questions, playing games of recognizing or naming music, and matching music to words, pictures, or other sounds, are several ways to help children savor what their listening tells them.

Listening and reading

Listening to stories and being able to read are related. In many studies, early readers are reported to have heard books read aloud regularly when they were preschoolers.[36] Children's comprehension of spoken language and of written prose also are related; children who understand radio stories better have higher standardized reading scores.[37] (No such relationship is apparent between television comprehension and reading ability.) Why is learning to read associated with listening to literature?

Listening to language exercises mental skills also needed to read. In both activities, a child must concentrate on the orderly flow of language, identify words, interpret them in grammatical context, and remember their meaning. Such basic abilities help listener and reader alike when it comes to following a story or extracting its main points. If anything, listening tends to bias children's learning toward the gist or essential message of a story, whereas reading leads to better memory for verbatim details.[38] There is an added advantage in listening to literary language; because it follows more formal rules of grammar and vocabulary than ordinary conversation, the word patterns children hear listening to fiction approximate those they must deal with when reading.

The younger the child, and the less skilled in reading, the greater the potential payoff from prose listening. But what benefit accrues to listeners once they are fluent readers? Perhaps skilled readers proceeding at their own pace even understand more from a text than do listeners. Speech rate is an issue for radio listeners of any age; too fast or slow speech detracts from a story's effectiveness. Young children have definite preferences for speaking rate and have been found to favor slightly faster speech than older children and adults.[39] In fact, listening and reading skills usually even out with age. College students summarize stories equally well after listening or reading.[40] Admittedly, listening to stories is more luxury than skill developer among able readers, but I recommend making it a luxury you consider necessary.

Listening to stories also expands children's literary universe and may increase their incentive to read.[41] Young listeners can be introduced to literature far beyond their reading level; children entering first grade understand more words than they will learn to read in the first five years of school.[42] Prior exposure to a tale on record or radio will motivate some children to try reading the book. Audio productions that bring to life worthy characters and situations can stay with a child for life. They did for at least one Broadway playwright:[43]

> I listened to the radio. Shows like 'The Green Hornet' and 'The Lone Ranger' and 'Let's Pretend' appealed to the imagination. I had to make a theater in my head for those shows. I made a little stage for the Metropolitan Opera broadcasts every Saturday. I had little figures of Rigoletto and Aida. I'd move the scenery. To me, that was more real than life. I spent a great deal of time in my room with the door closed – but happy.

Few adults can point so clearly to an early media experience as a source of inspiration for later professional success. And time spent with the unobtrusive radio may be especially elusive to memory. But radio and audio permit a very personal response to storytelling which should not be neglected by children, who are just learning how to listen.

Hands on

Encourage children to listen to stories. It will help them appreciate not only language and literature, but the myriad of sounds that surround them.

What to listen to

Younger children   When selecting audio fiction for children, consider both subject matter and production quality. The younger the child, the more important it is to find stories that make ample use of character voices, music and other sounds that help convey narrative meaning. The more well-placed sound cues the better. Not that a six-year-old should never hear prose read. But they will better understand – and perhaps sit still longer for – the fully dramatized story than narration. Remember too that the sound of words has more immediate impact than their meaning. That is why poems, songs and nursery rhymes make such good listening for young children.

Older children   School age listeners who are proficient with language can get more out of highly worded stories. They may especially enjoy language that plays with word sound and meaning, such as tongue twisters, riddles and homonyms (words that sound alike but mean different things, like horse and hoarse). Once we master any symbol system, language being just one, it is fun to experiment with and test its limits.

Familiarity   Children's listening is affected by familiarity with a story. It is easier to listen to a story you already know. Then, if you become distracted during the telling, you can more readily retrieve the story's thread and reconstruct the missing piece. Second time listeners are being reminded of a narrative, not first having to learn it. On the other hand, children who hear a story they have already seen on TV, in a movie, or in print, lose the opportunity to picture it first themselves.

When it comes to audio, familiarity with a story refers not only to the text, but to voices, music and other sounds. Hearing stories told by people children know and like adds to their appeal. Tape record yourself reading stories. Children may want to participate in the taping by playing the part of a character or making sound effects. This makes wonderful listening when children are at home by themselves.

When, where, and how to listen

Locating conducive conditions for story listening is winning half the battle. Consider children's schedules in light of what you know about story listening – that it demands concentration, that there is nothing to look at, that other sounds will compete for their attention. Story listening suggests quiet times and places where children's movement is already restricted. Time spent traveling in the car, for instance, offers ripe occasions for bringing along a battery-powered tape recorder and a few tapes. How about listening to adventures in far-off places en route to the supermarket? Passengers can listen together or a child can use earphones and listen alone. Listening to stories also can be a refreshing alternative to watching TV for children home sick in bed. The bathtub makes ideal terrain in which to safely heed the call of sea adventures. A little nook or cranny in the classroom can be outfitted for listening as well.

Occupying eyes and hands is part of the challenge facing listeners. The easiest solution is to listen in the dark. Spooky stories are the best, although children may prefer hearing them with other people around. Once lights are on, however, young listeners may not be content to just sit and gaze off into space. Another approach is to make materials available for youngsters to look at and handle during a broadcast or recording. They may be related to the narrative, like the storybooks that often accompany records and tapes. These booklets can improve listening comprehension by offering a printed or picture version of the story. But children also like using materials unrelated to a story while they listen. They can elaborate on a story's content as they please with the help of paper, pencils, play figures, clay and building sets. Reversing the emphasis, an audio drama can be used to motivate an art project. Painting to music, sound effects, even a narrated story, can evoke a special mood and spark imaginations.

Ear play

(1) Voice experiments

- Repeat the same words in different character voices. Example: say 'This soup is delicious, isn't it?' as a wicked witch, a prissy grandmother, a small child.

- Try intending different meanings each time. Sound suspicious, sincere, enthusiastic.

- Have children describe each utterance. What kind of character are you pretending to be? How does this character feel?

- Switch roles. Have children experiment with their voices for other listeners' benefit.

- Choose messages for them to practice reciting from newspapers, product packages and commercials, recipes, as well as from stories.

(2) 'Mystery Sound' game

- Borrow a sound effects record from the library.

- After each sound, have children guess its source. Encourage children to describe sounds fully.
- Award credit for each correctly identified sound and a prize to the best sound detector.

As alternatives to the sound effects recording:

- Take turns making sounds somewhere out of sight but within earshot.
- Most sound effects involve movement: rustle paper, drip water, brush your teeth. Kitchens are full of sound-making tools and appliances. See whether subtle differences in your own movements or in objects used can be distinguished.
- Sound-making equipment must be put away after use!
- Have children try voicing sounds. Use Fred Newman's book *Zounds: The Kids' Guide to Sound Making* (Random House, 1983).
- Have children make up a story that uses a different voice or sound for each character.

(3) 'Scavenger Sound Hunt'
- Make a list of five to ten sounds audible around the house, neighborhood or school. Include easier ones for seven- to eight-year-olds, more obscure ones for older children.
- Send children out with list, tape recorder and blank tape cassette.
- See if they can locate and record all sounds listed.
- Have children take turns if recorders are scarce. Some public libraries lend out tape recorders.

Chapter 3

Why read children picture books?

No one need approach reading aloud a picture book with trepidation. Perhaps no one does. Television assumes center stage as storyteller for most children in America today. But hearing a picture book read aloud has its own allure. And like a nutritious dessert, it satisfies both child and adult.

To radio's voicing of a tale, we first add pictures. Illustrations are allies, especially to young readers. Picture content is accessible and pleasing to look at. Instead of straining their listening attention, children can lean on pictures' silent, yet vivid messages to help them visualize and interpret a plot. And surely illustrations motivate children to thumb through, even read a book themselves. As an older child reading books already thin with pictures, I can remember waiting, waiting, and peeking ahead for the illustrated pages to come up.

The book itself is another lure. Unlike radio broadcasts, which rather like ghosts come and go without being seen, books are real objects. A child can hold, hug, smell, and alas chew on a picture book. While the same claim of tangibility may be advanced on behalf of audio cassettes, records, video cassettes and film, the only story immediately visible to a child is the one inside a book's covers.

Finally, add a live reading and possibly a lap. Being read a story by someone in person, up close, imparts to literature a human dimension still beyond the reach of modern technology – that is, until robots come padded and heated. The reader is a story's agent, not another audience member. Being in this position makes a big difference. Now you determine how the story is delivered, with what character voices, sound effects, pacing and expression. Presenting a story to children entails giving more of yourself.

Reading picture books to children is easy to endorse intuitively. Let's examine what educational and psychological substance there is to this advocacy.

The case against pictures

Popular though they may be, illustrations have been shown to interfere with children's prose reading. Although we are mainly concerned here with being read *to*, children hearing a book read aloud may try reading it themselves.[1] As a parent or teacher, one expects that exposing children to picture books and other illustrated stories will improve their reading ability. Some account of this negative evidence is therefore warranted.

Problems with pictures arise when children first learn to read. Imagine kindergarteners trying to decode simple words (boy, bed, man, car) either with or without an identifying picture above each one. At first, youngsters who see pictures name more words correctly. But then the pictures are removed, and with only the print before them children are asked to give the word names again. Now those five-year-olds with no previous access to pictures perform better.[2]

Why might pictures interfere with acquiring a sight vocabulary? Let's analyze the task. To recognize a word, one must look at, discriminate, and remember the arrangement of letters. Illustrations that picture the word are not relevant to that process. Time spent looking at the picture is time taken away from studying the word. Moreover, children can guess the word name from looking at the picture instead of the printed label; producing an answer from the picture cue requires less effort.

Pictures also disrupt children's prose reading when they present conflicting information to that of the text. Mismatches between text and pictures – such as the word 'cat' shown with a drawing of a lemon (!) –

cause second and third graders to read more slowly and make more mistakes than when there are no accompanying pictures.[3] This interference occurs even when students have been warned that the pictures will trick them and should be ignored.

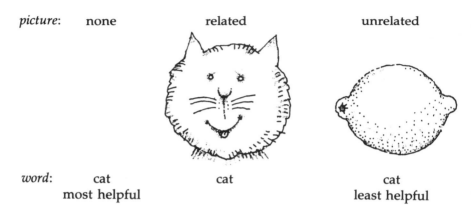

picture: none   related   unrelated

word: cat   cat   cat
         most helpful   least helpful

Figure 3.1: Decoding new words

Perhaps you are thinking such a situation is unrealistic. After all, no sane publisher of children's books would deliberately mismatch text and pictures. Such mischievousness could only be the work of demonic experimenters. But even when illustrations are carefully related to the text, they may depict diverse, complex story content. When the task is deciphering words, pictures don't always help. If a child comes to a word he or she already knows, then the picture is superfluous. A youngster who doesn't know a word and looks to the illustration for a clue to its identity may be misled by unrelated things in the picture.[4] We begin to see how critical is the relationship between picture and text.

These findings point up something else. Younger and less skilled readers are more susceptible to the distracting effects of pictures. It stands to reason: for beginning readers, picture content is more available than the meanings of many words. As a result, pictures can modify young readers' naming of words just as words can modify their naming of pictures. When pictures and prose are contradictory, even fourth graders answering questions about a story have been found to favor picture information over that in the text.[5] This symmetry disappears as reading level rises; words still influence picture naming, but the converse is no longer true.

Another very different argument against illustrating stories is based on the value of having children form their own images. As psychoanalyst Bruno Bettelheim has explained: 'a fairy tale loses much of its personal meaning when its figures and events are given substance not by the child's imagination, but by that of an illustrator.'[6] While there is wisdom in this observation, there also is more to be observed. These days many people glibly accuse highly visual media, and television more than books, of inhibiting children's creativity. Rarely are these media credited for inspiring new images. The influence that pictured stories have on children's imagery cannot be so easily dismissed, and I have devoted chapter 6 to this subject.

The case for pictures

Alice was beginning to get very tired of sitting by her sister on the bank, and of having nothing to do: once or twice she had peeped into the book her sister was reading, but it had no pictures or conversations in it, 'and what is the use of a book,' thought Alice, 'without pictures or conversations?'[7]

Appeal With this absolute recommendation of books with pictures and dialogue, Lewis Carroll initiates *Alice's Adventures in Wonderland*. Alice's disinterest in her sister's reading material suggests one of illustrated books' touted virtues, their appeal. There is a pervasive belief that children are more attracted to books that have pictures. Unfortunately, there are few published studies comparing the eagerness with which children approach illustrated or unillustrated editions of a text. Pictures also are credited with increasing children's enjoyment of books. And in fact, one group of second graders presented stories with or without accompanying drawings did voice preferences for the illustrated versions.[8] Admittedly, such findings have a ho hum quality. Well, you may say to yourself, what sighted second grader wouldn't favor a story that has pictures? What would be more interesting to know is whether this preference diminishes as children get older and become more competent readers.

There is little felt need to document what most people think is self-evident. Clearly, children can see some of what goes on in a story by looking at the pictures. Illustrations make stories accessible to very young children, whereas words do not unless someone else is reading. Children's facility for inferring meaning from pictures gives the illusion they are learning in no time, it seems so easy. That is where the case for pictures' appeal rests: with such limited research, it must be accepted on intuitive grounds, and not unreasonably so.

Reinforcing meaning In contrast, that the addition of pictures improves what children remember and understand of stories is well documented. The claim most often researched is: children learn better the story content that appears in both pictures and text. As the schematic diagram in Figure 3.2 shows, story information can be given in words, pictures, or both. In a typical study, primary grade girls and boys listen to an unfamiliar narrative passage read aloud. Some students also see line drawings that visualize important content. Then all children are asked questions to test their story knowledge. See example 1 on page 38. The addition of related pictures generally improves children's oral story recall by at least 40 percent,[9] a dramatic endorsement for reading children picture books.

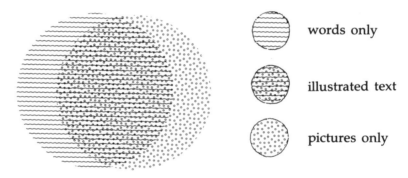

words only

illustrated text

pictures only

Figure 3.2: Information sources, illustrated books

Now when listening to a story, looking at pictures is a complementary activity. But remember how looking at pictures competed with learning to read, both being visual tasks. This raises the question: does adding relevant pictures aid learning from stories when children are doing the reading? In general, it does. Whether answering questions or retelling an entire plot, children as late as sixth grade better understand the fiction they read when its major content is illustrated.[10]

Whether pictures help or hinder prose learning therefore depends not only on how well pictures relate to the text, but on what is being learned. Learning to decipher a word is one thing, knowing what it means quite another. In the latter case, identifying pictures are a big help. Pictures promote children's story understanding when they depict information central to both the text and the tasks put to children.   •

How do pictures help here? When pictures and text are said to overlap, it implies that information is repeated. Perhaps these illustrations enhance children's story learning by simply restating the message. Two researchers devised a simple experiment to test this possibility. One group of children listened to a story and saw its illustrations, the other group listened twice. If repetition of content is all that's responsible for this picture enhancement effect, they reasoned, then performance in the two groups should be equal. But it wasn't. Comparing children's recall of story information, the picture group still learned more than the listeners, although the gap in performance was reduced by about half.[11]

Even when story illustrations are redundant with the text, they do more than reiterate verbal content. As symbols, pictures and words provide different access routes to fiction. Once a story is illustrated, children can remember its images as well as its words; it can be dually encoded.

Adding meaning This brings us closer to the heart of the case for picture books. The less often researched but stronger claim made for pictures is: children learn better from stories when pictures contribute new information important to the overall message. (This is 'pictures only' information in Figure 3.2.)

Figure 3.3: How pictures help children understand stories (copyright © 1970 by Gail E. Haley)

(1) *Verifying the text*:

Read in text	He crept through the tall grasses. . . .
Test story recall	What did Ananse creep through?
See in picture	Yes, there he is 'creeping' through tall grasses.

(2) *Clarifying the text*:

Read in text	Next Ananse cut a frond from a banana tree. . .
Test story comprehension	What is a frond?
See in picture	That leaf he's holding could be a frond.

(3) *Organizing the text*:

Read in text	He crept . . . till he came to the nest. . . .
Test picture recall	Where is the nest?
	Where is Ananse in relation to the nest?
See in picture	The nest hangs from a tree branch. Ananse is near – in right foreground of – the tree. The nest is on the tree's left.

(4) *Adding meaning*:

Read in text	No reference.	
Test picture recall	What does the tree look like?	
See in picture	Literal:	It has dark crooked branches and no leaves.
	Simile:	It's branches look like an old man's knobby knees.

To test what children learn from illustrations, a story is analyzed to sort out information only in the pictures: in Gail Haley's illustration for *A Story a Story* on page 37, examples of such content are the nest's location and the spider man Ananse's appearance. Occasionally, plots related entirely in pictures are used. After a story is presented, children are asked questions the answers to which are found only in the pictures: they may be straightforward, such as 'Where is the nest?' or involve making inferences that can be based on a picture, such as 'How old is Ananse?' and 'How do you know?' Children's retellings also may be scored for references to picture content.

Research evidence confirms that children understand and remember story information present only in the illustrations. In fact, they remember picture content longer than they do the verbal text.[12]

Children's grasp of pictured story content is all the more impressive when you consider that it usually is tested verbally. Rarely are children provided visual means to display their picture knowledge: such methods include having children recognize pictures, put them in order, arrange story props, and draw. In chapter 6 we will look at samples of story content children have seen and then drawn from memory.

How do pictures help here? What kind of information do they add to the message? First, pictures add vividness to fiction by visualizing its characters, props and scenery. More than just enabling children to verify the text, by checking its correctness against the pictures, illustrations clarify the text by showing readers what its content looks like. The verb 'illustrate' means to make clear by example. This function is most conspicuous when pictures depict novel and fantastic story content. For instance, listening children's understanding of such unfamiliar vocabulary as 'frond' and 'calabash' in *A Story a Story* improved significantly when they saw illustrations picturing these objects.[13] See example 2 on page 38. With no visual referent, some listeners even mistook the hero, Ananse the Spider man, for a real spider or a girl named Nancy!

Pictures also add a spatial context for fiction. Laying out a scene on a page is like offering children a map of the story terrain. This information organizes the text by showing readers how things are arranged in space. See example 3 on page 38.

Both jobs – clarifying what things in stories look like and organizing where they are – emphasize a picture's economy of means. After all, a writer may describe a scene layout or a character's appearance. But in rendering this information, words and pictures differ dramatically in efficiency. How much more labored and less direct is the worded version. A picture is worth a thousand words because it delivers the visual image words only help us construct for ourselves.

Third, pictures add meaning to stories that is inexpressible in words. No amount of words, for example, can account for all the nuances of line, texture, color and composition that make a character visible in an illustration: Ananse's stoop and leanness, the length of his limbs, the shape of his skull. In fact, writers often evoke their clearest images by moving away from literal description to more abstract uses of language, such as metaphor and simile. See example 4 on page 38. In chapter 4 we will take a closer look at the meaningfulness and appeal to children of various story illustrations.

It is only worthwhile to speak on behalf of pictures for so long before feeling they must 'speak' for themselves. That is the point after all. Therefore I recommend to you the following three picture book illustrations, all of which fully exploit their narrative voice. The first is from *Anno's Journey*, by Mitsumasa Anno, a wordless adventure that follows Anno (the man on horseback) on his travels through Europe. The second example is from Maurice Sendak's *Where the Wild Things Are*. This

Figure 3.4 (copyright © 1977 by Fukiunkan Shoten Publishers)

Figure 3.5 (copyright © 1963 by Maurice Sendak)

Figure 3.6 (copyright © 1979 by Steven Kellog)

illustration provides a response to text from the previous page: 'And now,' cried Max, 'let the wild rumpus start!' The third page spread, from Steven Kellogg's *Pinkerton, Behave!*, also initiates an event in words and reacts in the picture. As is more common, however, text and picture appear together here. As you peruse these illustrations, notice how laden with information they are, yet how few words it takes to suggest an interpretation. You can see what a fine balancing act a good picture book is, as a narrative and artistic product!

Live voice, warm lap

Being read a picture book brings a story very close. This happens in several ways.

Being read a picture book is a less spare narrative treatment than listening to a story on radio or record. Once a story is illustrated, it occupies a visible space. Its presence is less remote; it takes on form, physical boundaries, even weight, if you count the feel of the book. (Holding a record, or a radio for that matter, fails to produce the same sense of connection with a story's substance. Try it and see for yourself.) Furthermore, as just discussed, pictures add another information source which improves children's story understanding.

Being read a picture book is a less solitary activity than witnessing a recorded tale. It necessarily involves children in a shared experience with another person, whereas listening to radio and watching TV do not. And even when a child listens to a story recording in the company of a parent or teacher, they both are audience members. Not so, however, when that adult assumes the more active role of presenting the story to a youngster; leaving the safety of the sidelines, an adult reader jumps into the performance ring.

Children's story learning seems to benefit from live narration. In one study, preschoolers were presented an illustrated story, half hearing a recorded narration, the other half a live rendition. Each child then retold the story in his or her own words. Children who heard the live narration included more words and main ideas than did those who heard the recording.[14] Such evidence suggests that more of the live message gets through to a four-year-old audience. We must be careful not to draw conclusions on the basis of one study's findings. But in our media studies at Harvard, live readings of the picture book *A Story a Story* also prompted primary grade students to include more poetic language in their accounts of the tale – not just 'the hornets' but 'the hornets-who-sting-like-fire' – than did a recorded narration.[15] If hearing prose helps children remember the sound and rhythm of language, then hearing it spoken in person may well heighten the effect.

Why should this be so? Children who hear a live story reading probably pay closer attention. Just being around young children, you may have noticed that the same girls and boys who wriggle restlessly with a storybook record perk up with interest when a live reader narrates a story. Recordings may deliver a less varied, less complex sound than the live human voice. Moreover, the highest fidelity recording cannot reproduce the warmth and visual interest that a person's presence supplies. It goes beyond voice.

Being read a picture book permits a less structured delivery than a recording or broadcast. A story in print is not fixed in time. Children read, or are read to, at no predetermined speed. Taking advantage of this flexibility, an adult reader adapts his or her pacing to the story, the child and the circumstance. The reader controls the story's flow; when he or she stops, so does the narrative action.

Children also can interrupt the narration, and they do. More children ask questions and offer comments while being read a story than while watching a televised version of the story with the same reader's voice on the sound track.[16] I first noticed this medium difference introducing six-to ten-year-olds to *A Story a Story* by either reading it to them individually or watching an animated version with them on TV. They asked for story-related information – 'Does he get stung?' – furnished observations – 'The other hornets are inside the nest' – and related story content to their own experience – 'I saw a bees' nest once.' Children kept volunteering such remarks even though I acknowledged them succinctly. The same thing happened when five-year-olds were presented a simple adventure story, Tomi Ungerer's *The Three Robbers*: live reading provoked more conversation than co-viewing.[17]

It is not that broadcast stories leave children mute, as you may know all too well. When children watch TV at home with friends or family, they often talk during the show.[18] But conversing interferes with paying attention to an ongoing story. Unless a program is familiar, something important may be missed while speaking. We therefore learn to fit television conversation into slow-moving dramatic moments and commercial breaks, or wait until later when our thought may be forgotten. One advantage of records, cassettes and other nonbroadcast formats is the greater control over a story's presentation they permit the audience; a child can easily stop, restart, or review a video cassette. And computer programs offer an even more flexible delivery.

Being read a picture book provides a training ground in how to use the medium. An adult who encourages conversation with a child during a picture book reading can model strategies for getting information out of illustrated books, as well as from a particular story. This education can begin very early, as soon as parents start looking at books with their children. In one case study, a researcher recorded thirteen conversations with her son that took place while reading Richard Scarry's *Storybook Dictionary*.[19] They read the book over a year's time, beginning when he was two and a half. She tried not just to read him the text but to stimulate his speech, by asking questions, 'What's that?' or 'What's happening?,' and by answering his inquiries. Analyzing their conversations, this parent-investigator observed that the role of who asked the questions shifted from mother to child. So did the role of who responded to questions, though this occurred later that year. By imitating his mother's questions and observations, this boy was learning a way to extract meaning from a picture book.

Finally, being read picture books encourages children to read. Numerous studies identify early readers as children who are read to on a regular basis.[20] And why not? Parents, teachers and librarians who read to children are preaching by their own example. Listening children can easily detect a narrator's enjoyment of a story. Enthusiasm is contagious.

Then there is the exposure to a selected book of fiction. As Jim Trelease pointed out in *The Read-aloud Handbook*, 'A child who is unaware of the riches of literature certainly can have no desire for them.'[21] Hearing a story read by someone a child loves infuses it with a certain warmth. Many adults remember with special fondness the stories that were read to them as children.

In these various ways, then, being read stories from picture books brings fiction close to children. To that end, an adult performs two important jobs: one is narrating the story, the other is responding to it as another audience member. Both roles offer endless opportunities to personalize fiction for children. There are as many reading styles as there are readers, and every reading is a live performance. As an audience member, a reader may raise or answer questions about a story, listen to children's comments, giggle, fume, even cry. This role of co-audience member is available to adults in other storytelling media. Reading children picture books just makes participating more convenient.

Reading versus telling

What distinguishes the stories told to children from those they are read is who knows the story by heart. Where a reader refers to a printed source, a teller refers to his or her memory. A storyteller is rather like a musician who no longer needs the musical score to perform a piece of music. As one notable storyteller explains, 'My responsibility is to know the story well enough to tell it from the heart (which is not the same as memorizing it – even if the text is actually remembered verbatim).'[22]

To learn a story, this teller first researches its background. Then she makes a chronological outline of the key events and begins to describe the story to other people. To better 'inhabit a story,' she also draws a map of the setting and the main character's actions within it. Different tellers rehearse a story in different ways: telling it to a mirror, telling it to a tape recorder, telling it over the sound of a radio or other distraction.

A performing storyteller offers a visual focus for children's attention. As such, telling occupies a curious position among media, somewhere between an unillustrated format, like a recording of the storytelling, and one that pictures story content literally using artwork or actors. Just how visually evocative a told story is depends as much on the performance as on the prose. Some tellers use gesture and facial expression to help an audience envision a story's landscape, events and personalities. Others fill in story images with sound, as when a teller imitates sound effects or performs to music. These matters of style and custom make a telling elaborate or spare.

Storytelling warrants mention even though I know of no studies evaluating what, specific to the medium, children learn from these experiences. To practice speculating about media effects for a moment though, what is the most distinctive and consistent feature of storytelling? I say individual live performance. My guess is that children who regularly attend storytelling sessions learn something about delivering a story orally: about using their voice, about handling themselves before an audience, about applying memorable tricks of the telling trade.

Storytelling warrants mention out of respect not for its age, venerable though it is, but for its simplicity. It is within reach of any one of us to tell children a story. No equipment is needed, not even a book. There is nothing to plug in. Telling children stories is worth trying, if you haven't already. It is the most direct route we have for bringing children fiction.

Hands on

Karla Kuskin, an author and reviewer of children's books, reminisced one Sunday (November 15, 1981) in *The New York Times*:

> Those were the days when a channel was simply a deep waterway, sesame was only a seed and people read aloud for entertainment.

Reading aloud still is a wonderful pastime. All you need is a willing child, appropriate reading materials, and a little time and energy.

Introducing young children to the library

Think about it: here is a place where all kinds of books are available for anyone in the community to look at and enjoy, even to take home and read. What a generous resource is the public library!

Introduce children to the library when they are young, indeed before they can read. Make a visit there something to get excited about, like a treat or reward. Ideally, plan trips to the library when you have an hour to spare. That way there will be enough time to browse through the bookshelves, read several picture books, and select books to borrow. But don't bring a rigid agenda. Make it easy. Take turns with your child choosing books to read. Each of you will probably find different books appealing. Many children's

45

reading rooms are equipped with other amusements, such as toys, games, dolls and building blocks. At the beginning, it is important for young children to associate the library with a pleasant experience, one they want to repeat. Most of all, you are instilling a positive attitude.

One substantive task you do have is teaching young children how to behave in a library. *The most basic rules of the library are*:

(1) Don't eat the books. A book is to read, not chew or tear up. A book is something to be careful with. We turn pages one at a time.

(2) No tantrums, please. A library is a quiet place. We talk softly so other people can read.

(3) Every book has its place. We don't replace a book anywhere on the shelf; it goes back where we found it or out on the table. Then it won't get lost.

(4) Books can be borrowed. We can take library books home to read. When the time is up, we need to return them. But we can pick out other books to borrow.

Be patient. A preschooler won't remember all these instructions right away. Practice them by visiting the library often. You are making an investment that will serve your children well all their lives.

Tips on reading to children

Delivery   What makes narration expressive is a reader's engagement with the story. The more a reader appreciates a narrative, the more effectively she can communicate what it has to offer. A good reader also uses her voice, modulating its pitch, strength, phrasing, pacing and the like, to suit the flow and meaning of the text.

Let me assume the narrator's role and show you what I mean. The hornet episode in Gail Haley's book *A Story a Story* (Atheneum, 1970) will supply us with examples. Please read through the text first to become familiar with the scene.

> Next Ananse cut a frond from a banana tree and filled a calabash with water. He crept through the tall grasses, sora, sora, sora, till he came to the nest of Mmboro, the hornets-who-sting-like-fire.
>
> Ananse held the banana leaf over his head as an umbrella. Then he poured some of the water in the calabash over his head.
>
> The rest he emptied over the hornet's nest and cried: 'It is raining,

raining, raining. Should you not fly into my calabash, so that the rain will not tatter your wings?'

'Thank you. Thank you,' hummed the hornets, and they flew into the calabash – fom! Ananse quickly stopped the mouth of the gourd.

'Now, Mmboro, you are ready to meet the Sky God,' said Ananse. And he hung the calabash full of hornets onto the tree next to the leopard.

When Ananse 'crept through the tall grasses, sora, sora, sora,' I slow down to let him creep and quiet down to let him sneak up on his unsuspecting victims. To me, his subsequent invitation to the hornets, 'Should you not fly into my calabash . . .?,' sounds sly and overly zealous. In contrast, the hornets' reply seems breathy and innocent: 'Thank you. Thank you.' And I cannot resist humming the word 'hummed.' The next moment they are captured: 'and they flew into the calabash – fom!' I push out the word 'flew' to move them in quickly. Punctuation offers clues to phrasing and emphasis. The dash after 'calabash' interrupts, so I pause, before the exclamation 'fom!' Now they cannot escape. That's that.

Every story reading is a personal effort. Let your own interpretation be your guide. Reach for a story's meaning when you read aloud and listen to the sounds words make. Also try and be sensitive to your listeners; adapt your narration to their interests too. That's really all it takes.

Discussion   It is tempting to plan entire lessons around fiction, it is food for so much thought. Such a systematic approach is sometimes just the thing; in school, stories are cornerstones for excellent lessons in language arts, social studies, science, history and art. More often, however, picture book readings take place amid the informality of a library, a doctor's office, or a bedroom. Therefore the following suggestions for talking about stories with children can be selected from, amplified, rearranged, or omitted at the reader's discretion. There are circumstances when a book cries out to be discussed, it so provokes listening children. At other times, a book is best left unprobed. After a deeply moving story, both reader and listener may want to savor their feelings, not analyze them; conversation can always be initiated after a rereading.

Suggestions for discussing stories

(1)   Repeat children's comments to acknowledge and verify what they have to say.

(2)   Ask for information to find out what children understand about a

story.

- 'What is that?'
- 'What is happening?'
- 'What will happen next?'
- 'Where? When?'
- 'Why?'
- 'How does a certain character feel?'

(3) Ask for opinions, likes and dislikes. Ask about:
- how picture content looks
- a character's behavior
- a story's ending.

(4) Point out things for children to notice in both the verbal text and the pictures.

(5) Offer information.

(6) Offer opinions.

(7) Relate story content to children's experience. One approach is to compare story content and real-life experience. Use real items to make comparisons vivid and fun. After reading *A Story a Story*, a reader and child might look at a hornets' nest, identify modern alternatives to calabashes, or cook yams for dinner.

Chapter 4

Children's illustration preferences

Watching young children browse the bookshelves in a library or store can discourage the most optimistic author, English teacher, or other lover of the printed word. One quick glance at the cover art seems to be all that many children need to decide which book to pick up, and which to discard.

What makes a picture appeal to children? We know that illustrations offer young readers access to a story's meaning. Do children savor pictures for their recognizable content alone? Is the kindergartener whose favorite book character is redheaded, tall, funny-looking, and wears patterned pants aware of a figure's color, scale, humor and detail? Children's opinions about pictures may simply be a matter of personal preference. Yet that preference is affected by age and education about art.

Understandably preoccupied with our offspring becoming literate, we tend to minimize the importance in their early reading experiences of looking at and enjoying the accompanying pictures. But discovering what children appreciate about story illustrations helps us to choose reading material that will cultivate their taste for images as well as for prose. After all, illustrated fiction often introduces children not only to literature but also to the visual arts: itself an important goal.

Picture biases of youth

What children find relevant about aesthetic objects changes over time. Being young and naive is associated with certain reactions to visual art, at least in most Western cultures.

Subject matter I have often heard educators advise adults who are bringing young visitors to the art museum: show them pictures that tell a story. This is wise counsel. The subject matter or content dominates young children's talk about art, as if they read a painting as a picture of a thing before seeing it as a statement expressive of artistic style, mood, social comment, or the like.[1] (The skill of recognizing a familiar item represented in two dimensions seems to come naturally: it doesn't depend on exposure to pictures. Infants five months old can distinguish an object from its picture, and a color photograph from a line drawing.[2]) Subject matter also largely determines younger children's choice of picture art. Most of all, kindergarteners' picture preferences suggest the kinds of people, animals and things they find interesting and the surroundings in which they like to imagine themselves active.[3] Young boys and girls tend to relate picture content to their own experience – 'I like to play with soldiers' or 'It looks like my dog'; in this respect, they embrace art in a very personal, egocentric way.

Realism Most children go through a stage from age seven or eight to at least nine or ten where they measure a picture's success by its resemblance to reality. The more like a photograph of its subject a painting is, the more likely it will be valued by children in this literal mind set.[4] (Some people never outgrow this orthodox stance toward art.) Children apply this criterion to their own artwork too, striving to render scenes they draft as realistically as possible. The range of subject matter they consider suitable for artists to portray expands with their interests and experience; for example, older children are more tolerant than younger ones of sad or unpleasant scenes. But what counts as acceptable execution of a work of art if anything becomes more restricted: color must be realistic, details historically correct, scale and proportions convincing. Abstract art and art that distorts reality for expressive purposes are very difficult for many children this age to swallow. In a way, their reaction to art has become less personal; now they are equipped with a more conventional standard for judging the literal 'truth' of a work of art. In the process, however, they begin to notice and admire the skill, time and effort artists bring to their work. Learning to separate technique from depicted content is an important step in aesthetic development.

Relativism Near adolescence, children loosen their strict demand for realism, and various styles and degrees of distortion and abstraction become more acceptable.[5] Although personal interest may always steer viewers toward certain art objects and away from others, children realize as they get older that anything can be the subject of good art. Teenagers will judge a painting on its more formal merits, including the artist's style, the way its content is arranged or composed, and how effectively the work conveys a message, mood, or feeling. They are more aware that artists intend their work to make a statement, and are curious about how certain rendered effects are achieved. In short, it is not until adolescence that most children become concerned with picture characteristics usually valued as artistic by adults.

Counter evidence: age isn't everything

Like beauty, art is in the eye of the beholder. For a picture to function aesthetically for the viewer, it must be enjoyed for more than what it represents and beyond its literal meaning. A picture's unique expressiveness comes in the way its lines form shapes and textures, in its use of color, in its sense of balance, space and light. How else could so many paintings of similar landscape or still life scenes affect us so differently? If most children's experience of paintings follows the course just described, then is appreciation of pictures *as art* lost to them? Should we ignore the art museum for several more years and so avoid a disappointing visit? Thumbing through some colorful magazines might be just as satisfying for younger children. It certainly requires much less effort.

The fact is, despite what was said above, young children are equipped to notice more about pictures than their depicted content. Detecting children's sensitivity to aesthetic features of art seems to depend largely on how you decide to measure it. Asking a young child to pick a favorite painting from an assortment and to justify his or her choice generates talk mainly about subject matter. As long as picture art can be sorted or selected by subject, that is what will most engage children's attention. But remove the distraction of content, by presenting paintings with no recognizable subjects or with similar subjects (all still lifes, all portraits), and young children's observations change dramatically. First graders are as adept as sixth graders at discerning such elusive concepts as artistic style; shown paintings by a single artist, children can often identify style well enough to choose another work by the same person.[6] Similarly, even five-year-olds can perceive the mood expressed in abstract paintings, by pointing to the pictures best described by words like happy, sad or excited.[7]

Most children also harbor preferences as to such formal features of pictures as color, composition and viewpoint. Younger children, for example, tend to choose highly saturated colors over diluted tints,[8] conventional perspective to more diagrammatic views,[9] and symmetrical compositions over other arrangements.[10] Although these aesthetic judgments are made out of context, they may still affect young people's opinions when they look at complex pictures.

Thus, even first graders are capable of perceiving a picture's form, style and expressiveness; under certain circumstances, they will make fine visual discriminations. Most of the time, however, children don't approach pictures so analytically. Should we intervene and encourage them to peruse pictures in a more sophisticated way? Training does affect perception. Youngsters educated in art or exposed to art tend to bring a more precocious eye to pictures.[11] On the other hand, if we just wait, children's opinions about art are likely to develop on their own. And even without adult intervention, youngsters with special aptitude in visual art may arrive at less conventional views toward pictures than their peers.[12]

Deciding the place of the visual arts in children's lives warrants every parent's and teacher's reflection. But before discussing the issue any further, let's come closer to everyday surroundings and see what happens when children are in the company of story illustrations.

Choosing story illustrations

How do children pick their favorite pictures out of books? In particular, what about cases where the same story has been illustrated many times? As just reported, comparing pictures with similar subject matter seems to free young children to take other features into account. But since the illustrations in a story carry such important information, perhaps considerations about picture content will still override other criteria they might use.

Children did just that kind of comparing in a study I conducted using Aesop fables. (Illustrators have been interpreting the fables of Aesop for over five hundred years now, and it is said that the history of the printed illustrated book can be shown by their work alone.[13]) Participating in this research were public school students ages five, eight and eleven. Fifteen children at each age were individually read five fables.[14] After hearing each tale, listeners chose among alternative illustrations the one they liked best and least to go with each story and gave reasons for their selections. I also asked children to judge the illustrations for specific features including realism, humor and appeal to other children and adults.

The reasons children offered for their picture preferences were scored to answer two general questions. First, what content do youngsters single out in choosing a fable illustration? Do they focus on only one character, on two characters in relation to each other, on the background, or instead on the picture as a whole? Are children talking about a character's appearance, actions, thoughts and feelings, or juxtaposition to props and scenery? Second, what about this content do they like or dislike? For instance, are children commenting about a picture's color, detail, size, or technique? Do they pick an illustration because it's funny or looks real or simply because it pictures something they like? Children's reactions to three of the fables follow.

'The Lion and the Mouse'   In this fable a mouse whose life is spared by a lion later rescues the same king of beasts from a hunter's net. Shown here are the four black and white illustrations children saw. Which picture do you think was the favorite among five-year-olds, eight-year-olds, or eleven-year-olds? Which one did children reject? Take a minute to consider your own feelings about each illustration. Which one do you like best?

Children's favorite pictures at all three ages were the engraving (4.3) and the small pencil drawing (4.1). Note that three hundred years' time separating the two artists' work was of no apparent consequence in children's decision making; the engraving dates from 1665, the pencil sketch from 1979. The larger pencil close-up (4.2) was the consistent second choice. The pen and ink (4.4) was the least liked illustration, with older children more likely to disapprove. Eleven-year-olds' picture preferences tended always to be the most clear-cut and homogeneous, kindergarteners' the most varied.

What motivated these selections? The engraved illustration certainly won the majority vote as most realistic. Further, as we might suspect, older children usually credit the most realistic rendering as being the work of the best artist. But if realism is so primary a criterion at this age,

Figure 4.1

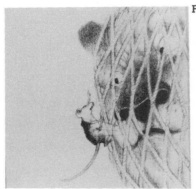

Figure 4.2

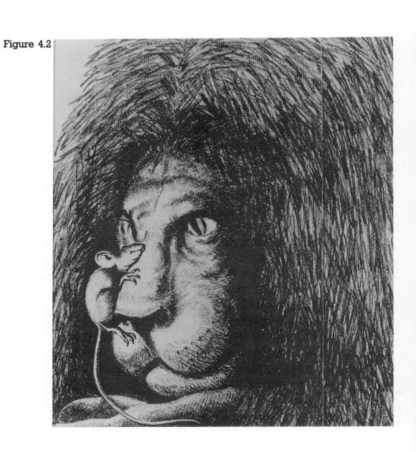

Figure 4.4

why didn't even more of them pick this picture first? Perhaps because it rarely produced a humor vote or even a smile, whereas the small pencil drawing was thought to be funny and also best at showing how both the lion and mouse were feeling. Then again, the two less popular examples were also perceived as funny, especially by eight-year-olds. Clearly, children's motives are not accounted for simply.

Children draw upon many kinds of observations to justify their picture selections. Older children do often base a choice on an illustration's realism: 'It [4.3] looks the reallest.' But the great majority of comments lie elsewhere. In choosing the engraving, for example, children also referred to form: 'I like how the lion's teeth are formed, really sharp' (age 5); technique or possibly line quality: 'I like how the lion's fur is made' (age 5); action: 'It has more action in it' (age 8); character emotion: 'You can see the lion's angry; it shows his emotion' (age 11); and setting: 'It has pretty things in it, trees, flowers . . .' (age 8). One cautious kindergartener pointed to the lion and reported with obvious relief: 'He's caught in the net.' Reactions like that and this one, 'I like when the lion's in the net and can't scratch people,' attest to the power young children assign lifelike pictures of dangerous animals.

If children admire this engraving's highly realistic rendering, ferocious-looking but contained lion, and country scenery, they enjoy the small pencil drawing (4.1) for other reasons. In particular, children were struck by the cooperative relationship they had heard described between the two characters and saw depicted here: 'The lion's scared . . . and the mouse is saying "I'm gonna help you" ' (age 11). Some children felt this content was especially true to the story text: 'The little one helped the big one. It's the moral of the story, it's important!' (age 11). Fans of this picture also appreciated its humor: 'The mouse is acting funny; it's not regular for a mouse to go' (child points his index finger and giggles), or 'The mouse is talking to a lion; it's funny' (both age 8).

The larger pencil illustration (4.2) evoked some similar positive reactions from the children: 'It looks like they're friends' (age 11) or 'I like the mouse hugging the lion on the nose; it's funny' (age 5). Close-ups have a way of drawing the young viewer into a more intimate scene. But the warmth and humor observed in this drawing by some children were offset by complaints from others: 'The lion has too much hair up there' (age 5), 'The lion's fur is so black' (age 8), or 'His eyes look scary' (age 5).

For an illustration to please older children, it must depict its story content accurately and convincingly. Otherwise they will deride it for violating story facts and logic. This was a problem with the pen and ink illustration (4.4) which was rejected for its cartoon-like style, but even more vigorously for its implausibility: 'The lion was caught in a net, not these strings of spaghetti' or 'He doesn't look caught in a net; it's just a bunch of rope he's tangled up in' (both age 11).

Part of what guides children's illustration choices, then, is how expressively and dramatically characters are portrayed. The more stouthearted youngsters were engaged by the fierce lifelike lion in (4.3). Indeed, children rarely referred to the mouse in this picture except to comment about how hard it was to find. (It's in the bottom right corner.) Mellower souls appreciated the more sympathetic and amusing treatment of the two characters in (4.1). The mouse figured as a more important character in children's comments here; its prominent position in the picture helps compensate for its smalll size.

'The Country Mouse and the City Mouse' In this second fable, a city mouse unimpressed with its country cousin's simple ways invites its relative to see the city. But the danger they face there convinces the country mouse its rural life is better: 'I would rather have my plain meal in my quiet hole than feast like this in fear of my life.' The three illustrations children chose among to accompany this story appear in Figures 4.5, 4.6 and 4.7. Although reproduced here in black and white, the children saw them in color.

Picking a favorite illustration for this fable proved difficult, since many children liked all three candidates. However, half the children chose the watercolor (4.5), and more older children preferred it. This choice surprised me, given that another illustration (4.6) was considered the most realistic effort.

Once again, a realistic style was not the sole basis for children's illustration selections. If anything, the eleven-year-olds chose the watercolor (4.5) illustration for its fanciful treatment of the subject. Their defense of this picture reveals an appreciation for the match between a story's reality or fantasy status and that portrayed by the artist: 'They look like the real people mice in the story' or 'Since the mice talk, they should look more like people.' Consistency with the fable's content also was perceived in details of characters' appearance such as costumes: 'The city mouse has on fancy clothes like he should, the country mouse has raggedy clothes' and facial expression: 'It shows the city mouse's face – "the city's so great, the country's nothing" '. Furthermore, this picture seems best at helping children distinguish between the two characters. Not only can they tell the mice apart, but they are more likely to assign different emotions to each one: the city mouse seems to them proud or

Figure 4.5

Figure 4.6

Figure 4.7

happy, his country cousin, most of all, surprised. In comparison, the scenes of impending danger in the other two illustrations suggest two frightened mice to most children.

Eight-year-olds imposed the strictest reality testing on their picture selections. They often made the smaller painterly illustration (4.6) their first choice on such grounds: 'It looks the most real' or 'The mice look like mice.' Occasionally, a child struggled to have a picture (4.6 in this case) satisfy both fictional and real-world standards: 'The country mouse wouldn't have anything on but fur. But then *most* mice don't wear neckties' (mouse on the right has on a tie). However, children this age observed many other features in deciding which illustration they preferred. Choosing (4.5) for example, one boy offered this rich explanation: 'It's simple to see. It has hard lines. It shows their feelings well too; see, the city mouse is being a show-off.'

Most kindergarteners' interest in these illustrations had to do neither with realism nor accurate interpretation of the story. It pertained instead to their appetites. Seeing appealing foods pictured was sufficiently distracting to guide many five-year-olds' illustration choices. They simply picked the picture with the best-looking goodies: (4.5) – 'Hot dogs are hanging all over the place, mmmn;' (4.7) – 'I love grapes or blueberries or whatever they are;' and (4.6) – 'I like cherries' or 'It looks like good cake.' One child summed up the attraction as follows: 'Anything with cake, I look!' Younger children praised pictures as well for such traits as size, – 'I like the teeny mice,' 'pretty colors;' costumes – 'They're all dressed up;' and characters' physical closeness – 'They're snuggling together.' Nonetheless, having food visible led many young children aesthetically astray. I wish I had kept track of how close to lunchtime each child's interview was.

Many children rejected illustrations which failed to fulfill these same criteria. We find kindergarteners taking issue with a picture showing food they dislike: 'I don't like cheese' (4.5) and eight-year-olds objecting to an illustration looking 'too cartoony' (4.5). Eleven-year-olds discredited illustrations for not satisfying their story expectations: 'You never see mice dress in that kind of stuff [4.7]; if they dressed at all, their clothes would be more like these' (pointing to 4.5), or 'It [4.6] looks like the real thing; it's not as much fun to look at.'

At all ages, some children disapproved of pictures on formal grounds, including too little color, the wrong colors, too many details (4.7), or a generally less pretty scene (4.6). Only one child, an eight-year-old, raised the issue of an illustration's age, rejecting (4.6), © 1918, in part because

'It looks old-fashioned. It's blurry.'

'The Wolf and the Crane'   In this last example, a crane saves a wolf from choking to death by extracting a bone stuck deep in its throat, but receives a disappointing reward in return for its efforts. Below are the two black and white illustrations children saw. Which picture do you prefer? Which one do you think the children will favor at each age?

Figure 4.8   Figure 4.9

Most children elected the small engraving (4.8) to accompany this fable rather than the line drawing (4.9). The first artist is credited as the better one and his illustration is seen to be prettier and more realistic.

The most heated conversation provoked by these two fable illustrations pertained to their artistic merit. These observations were fostered by presenting pictures similar in content, consistent with the text, yet so different in style. Older children's approval of the engraver's style, or really their objection to the other artist's technique, is what made this selection so decisive. From many eight- and eleven-year-olds' viewpoints, the artist's work in (4.9) simply proved inferior. For one thing, he drew too little: 'It's just an outline,' 'There's no fur or feathers on them,' or 'There's no background; there's nothing to tell where they are.' To make matters worse, what little he did include was thought to be poorly drawn: 'See the legs crossed? You shouldn't see those two lines,' 'You can see through it; it's invisible,' or, the ultimate insult, 'It looks like a kid drew it!'

Not all children participated in this criticism. There were a few older youngsters who, as with the choice of (4.5) for 'The Country Mouse and the City Mouse', favored a less realistic picture to illustrate a fable, as well as those for whom the line drawing (4.9) was the more readable: 'You can see everything when it's not colored in.' Moreover, kindergarteners were generally less vehement in their disapproval of the drawing, finding fault not so much with basic technique as with details like the droop of the bird's body: 'The feathers look like they're dead; you know, like flowers are dead' or the wolf's clenched teeth: 'This wolf's mouth is [child shuts her teeth tightly together].'

Developing taste

Kindergarteners and preteens are both full of opinions about picture art. Their age influences which pictures children do or don't like, not whether they harbor preferences. For example, older children are often sympathetic to a picture whose subject looks realistic, whereas younger children will reject the same picture if it depicts a violent or unpleasant scene in too lifelike a fashion – witness some kindergarteners' distrust of Figure 4.3's feisty lion. Furthermore, children's response to many features of pictures, such as color choices, detail, size, even humor, has less to do with their age than it does with their individual personalities and past exposure to art.

That young children respond so personally to pictures is noteworthy. Older children readily assume that 'little kids' (five-year-olds) will always choose the funniest, most cartoon-like picture to go with a fable. In fact, the youngest children voiced the most varied illustration preferences. Kindergarteners' reactions to illustrations were impressive in other ways too. They willingly praised and criticized pictures' formal features, except when picture content aroused their consumer passions. Young children were also careful to notice facial expressions, as if checking to see if a picture was friend or foe. Kindergarteners could identify the characters' feelings in each fable, when asked, although they used a limited vocabulary to label these emotions. A young child would say an animal felt 'sad' or 'bad,' while an older one might say he was 'worried' or 'depressed.' Where a young child would say, 'I don't like his mouth [tight-lipped, downturned],' an older counterpart inferred, 'He's starting to get mad.'

The illustrated stories young people choose to read not only reflect their current taste in literature and art. Picture fiction also shapes and exercises children's powers of observation. By helping to tell a story, illustrations by their very nature convey information children find of interest. Young readers will peruse illustrations to better understand and relish a story, whether or not they know how line, color, and composition contribute to their enjoyment of scenery, characters and conflict. Children's responses to Aesop fable illustrations suggest the wide range of data and minute detail that engages their attention. If anything, reactions to these terse, impersonal tales underrepresent the strong sentiments children entertain toward story illustrations.

Hands on

Sharing the artfulness of illustrated stories

Illustrated fiction offers an ideal context for introducing children to picture art. Start children young, while their responses to art are spontaneous, flexible and unfettered by concerns with realism and other artistic conventions.

Selecting illustrated stories   Expose children to all kinds of illustrations. There's tremendous variety to choose from in illustrated storybooks, picture books, pop-up books, board books, cloth books, etc. Take full advantage. You can familiarize children with many picture mediums, graphic styles and book formats. Later, when their taste becomes more selective, those early experiences may keep them in touch with pictures they might otherwise not revisit.

(1) Let children pick out their own books. If they're interested in a certain subject, indulge their curiosity by finding several stories on the topic. It also keeps you up-to-date with what they find appealing.

(2) Acquaint children with books of your choosing. On one library visit, you might select tiny books and oversized ones. Another day choose only books with black and white illustrations.

(3) For older youngsters, select more than one version of the same story, as in the fable study, and compare them for illustration style, page design, and even typeface. Be aware of the different media illustrators use, such as watercolor, pen and ink, cutouts and photography.

(4)   Pick out books both you and your children will enjoy looking at.

Talking over pictures   Do you ever wonder what your children notice in the book illustrations they scrutinize? Their perception of a picture is likely to differ from yours. Talking with children about what they observe in pictures is nonthreatening, yet it reveals their feelings and priorities. Most of the children I spoke with about Aesop fable illustrations or other story pictures seemed intrigued if not surprised to find an adult curious about their opinions. Apparently unpracticed in this sort of dialogue, they struggled to find words through which to share their impressions. Making pictures the subject of conversation is a habit worth cultivating. It will always be there as a pleasant, informative, even intimate way of spending time with your children.

Also let children know how you feel about the illustrations you view together. Most children I asked predicted adults would favor the most realistic, serious picture in an array. It was their best guess; they didn't seem to really know. Occasionally a girl or boy confidently pointed out a picture, remarking, 'My mom would like this one, it's pretty' or 'My grandpa would pick this one; he likes funny pictures.' Why shouldn't your children be aware of your taste? As long as you allow them their opinions, don't make yours a secret.

Here are some general questions to ask children about illustrations. Many more will likely occur to you, depending on the book you are looking at and the child you are with.

(1)   Which picture do you like the best? or
      Which one is your favorite picture?
      Why? What do you like about it?

(2)   Which one do you think is the worst picture?
      Why don't you like it? or What's wrong with it?

(3)   Which picture is the most ...
      - scary?   - colorful?
      - funny?   - exciting?
      - ugly?   - friendly?
      - quiet?   - sad?
      - messy?   - happy?
      - angry?   - peaceful?

(4)   Which picture (if any) would you like to pretend was real?
      or ... pretend you were in?

(5) Is there anything in this picture you don't understand?

(6) Is there anything in this picture that reminds you of . . .
- yourself?
- someone else you know?
- your house?
- somewhere else you've been?
- something you've seen on TV or in the movies?

Don't feel as if you have to correct children for mistaken views of art. The idea here is to help children discover how much there is to notice and feel about a picture.

Beyond story illustrations

Children's lives today are already filled with pictures. How deliberately you want to instruct children in aesthetic appreciation and sensitize them to picture composition, style and expressiveness depends a lot on your own experience with and attitude toward art. Some parents and teachers enjoy cultivating this aptitude in youngsters, while others feel ill-equipped to pass on this kind of information. But you will do children a real service to share picture art with them in whatever ways you can. Whether pointing out things in paintings for them to notice, asking their impressions of posters and ads, or joining them in savoring comic strip comedy, you help children learn to benefit from their time with pictures.

Picture sources
- Nonfiction books with lots of illustrations, both juvenile and adult. Select books of mutual interest whenever possible. Subjects might include: animals, aircraft, cars, costumes or fashion, sports, toys, dolls, television and art.

- Magazines with colorful illustrations. These can be publications intended for children, such as *Mad* or National Geographic's *World*, as well as periodicals that you like. They can be old or new.

- Newspaper comic strips. Pick one to follow together.

- Mail order catalogs. Simply flip through the pages with one or more children, letting everyone pick out items they do or don't like.

- Billboards, posters and ads on buses or buildings, store signs, graffiti, or other street graphics. Looking at advertisements together invites conversation about the many different ways pictures and graphics are used to promote products and services.

- Product packaging and labels.

- Old photographs.

- Postage stamps.

Visiting art museums Why not show children the finest examples of pictures available? Important paintings, drawings, prints and photographs displayed in art museums exploit artistic properties in the most excellent ways. Try and make regular, casual outings to the art museum. Like walks amid any varied and colorful landscape, museum visits can be a treat. Keep trips short and nondidactic. Children who feel at ease in art museums from an early age and have fond memories of their visits are more likely to make enjoyment of art part of their adult lives. When children are still young, pick out one or two galleries as the focus of a visit. Let older children help decide which areas in the museum they want to see. Even then, they will bypass many works. Consider your visits successful as long as a child gets excited about one piece of art and wants to return another day.

Hints for visiting art museums with children:

(1) Go on picture hunts. Start with simple items for children to find in pictures: 'Let's see how many . . . we can find.' Try searching pictures for animals, children, hats or shoes, weapons, faces, hands, or other things likely to appear in a group of pictures. Also try hunts organized around more formal themes: the picture with the most red, circles, shadows, the fanciest picture frame.

(2) Explore an art museum with older children in search of realistic art. Look for technical drawings, detailed engravings, pop art, photographs.

(3) Find examples for older children of a project completed in several steps, as when sketches are done before a painting is undertaken.

(4) Museum art that children may find appealing includes: Egyptian art, especially mummies; medieval armor and weapons; small carved figures of people and animals; and jewelry.

Chapter 5

No, but I saw the movie

When it comes to educating young audiences, moving pictures get a lot of bad press: television programs are too violent, movies are too sexual; commercials overly emphasize children's sweet tooth and end up causing cavities, movies overly excite their emotions and end up causing nightmares. 'Watching' is a nasty passive habit that robs children's time, imagination and ability to concentrate. Complaints against movies and TV as menaces to education seem louder and more plentiful than praise of their teaching virtues.

But what if content were not a problem, and more high quality fiction were produced for children on film and videotape, more carrots promoted than Cap'n Crunch cereal? What if time were not an issue either, and children occupied themselves equally with viewing and reading? Would many of us still feel more satisfied steering youngsters away from the screen? Is there something intellectually inferior about stories once their characters are shown moving through narrative space?

The moving picture

What do children learn from a movie or television show that they don't from a story in print? Consider how each medium tells its stories. Print fiction can explore the possibilities for human action, but the movements are at best mental images which the reader constructs out of words. Storybook illustrations can suggest or imply movement, as when figures are drawn with bent limbs,[1] even though each image remains static and discrete. In contrast, the illusion of movement is inherent in the continuous display of film and television images: when one still picture is quickly superseded by another, just slightly different one, the eye interprets the change as movement. Television, film, and animation differ in certain respects – the video image is less dense than film's, and the cartoon image is not live but drawn. Yet they all are able to project a dynamic image.

Character actions This change from printed page to moving picture affects story content. Moving pictures depict some parts of a plot more readily than others. Once pictures move, for example, we can see exactly what characters are doing. Dialogue, in comparison, relies much less on visible movement; in fact, talking on screen often requires that an actor slow down. A screenplay writer's job in many cases is to adapt story content originally in print to the screen's own production means.

The images and text below are from an animated film of the folktale *A Story a Story*. Now it is evident that Ananse 'held' and 'poured.' Compare these film frames with the book illustration that accompanies the same text, page 37. The cartoon visualizes more of the story's active verbs.

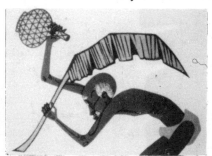

Figure 5.1   **Figure 5.2**

This visible behavior is not lost on children. Six- to ten-year-olds who saw this folktale as a televised cartoon reported more character actions in their story accounts than did youngsters presented the picture book.[2]

Viewers also mimicked more of what they saw charaters do.

In order to measure the impact of animation *per se* on children's learning, the two story versions being compared needed to be identical in other respects, such as their illustration style, text and narration. The film followed the book very closely; according to the director: 'we strive always for the result of the "picture book projected." '[3] Despite being such a strict test of medium differences, both younger and older children's memory for story events improved upon seeing characters in action.

Actions seen on film or television also are more memorable than those described verbally on radio, for story audiences of preschoolers[4] as well as fifth graders.[5] This learning bias holds up for sequences of events, too: preschool children recall the order of story events more accurately when the content is conveyed visually rather than in speech.[6]

Young viewers, however, do not necessarily use the story vocabulary to recall character actions. (Remember that children tend to recollect more of an author's specific wording after listening than after viewing.) For example, several children who watched *A Story a Story* on television described the moment pictured in Figures 5.1 and 5.2 using words like 'he sprinkled . . .' or 'he "shaked" some water on the banana leaf.' Considering that drops of water appear in the animated drawings (look closely), I am tempted to speculate that the choice of alternative verbs was not an error in recall, but instead based on what it really looked like Ananse was doing – not pouring water, but sprinkling it drop by drop. Further evidence of viewers' 'reading' from a remembered image is their literal account of where the water fell – not over his head, as the narrator says, but on the banana leaf.

Why is on-screen action more memorable for children? Filmed story events could conceivably be harder to absorb than those described in print or on radio: picture and sound both carry meaning, several events can take place at one time, and moving picture events progress at their own relentless pace. Although these aspects of on-screen action make absorbing a story a complex task, other features counterbalance.

Moving picture events can visually reinforce a verbal message. Children remember important television content better when it occurs in both speech and visible behavior, rather than in speech alone.[7] Still pictures help children's prose learning, and moving images are that much more plentiful. What characters do on screen, however, is not always consistent with or even commented on in words; there's rarely time for discussion in a fast-paced chase scene. Yet children remember well even those events not referred to in dialogue. Why? In part, it is greater attentiveness.

Visible movement catches the eye. Children of all ages pay more attention to the screen when there are high levels of physical activity.[8] On-screen action, accompanied often by sound effects and music, draws preschoolers' visual attention to television more predictably than violent content.[9] By comparison, children watch less when adults sit and talk quietly in front of the camera. Even if adults' conversation is about fighting, the actions they describe cannot be directly observed.

Also, a filmed performance of most actions is so lifelike that young viewers can easily recognize what's going on. Story content children understand will be easier for them to remember. When TV image and soundtrack are incompatible, it is the video content children favor;[10] pictures offer the path of less resistance to meaning.

Face value Moving pictures depict other narrative content that is optional in print and on radio.[11] A character seen on screen necessarily looks a certain way, dresses a certain way (unless an ugly duckling, black stallion, or unclad alien), and appears in certain surroundings. An individual's physical demeanor in a story, as in real life, hints at her age, health, social status, even personality. And that's standing still. Once she moves an eyebrow or feather, these gestures are symptomatic of her innermost thoughts and emotions – characters' behavior includes much more than just activity. An actress's image on screen can also be tampered with using close-ups, dramatic lighting, music and other production techniques.[12] Animation affords even more freedom to simplify or exaggerate a character's appearance. Yet when a cartoonist renders facial expression, he emphasizes the same features important in acting, the ones that move: eyes, mouth and eyebrows.[13] As we will see, even the subtlest trace of expression in an animated figure can carry emotional weight for a viewer.

| Happy | Sad | Angry | Suprised | Afraid |

Figure 5.3

Writers of fiction have more choice about including character description. A heroine's appearance can be delineated in meticulous detail or ignored. Unlike a heroine's irrepressible image on screen, her appearance on the printed page is elaborated only at the author's discretion. In fact, fiction writers sometimes are advised to avoid explanation entirely: 'A good writer can get anything at all across through action and dialogue, and . . . should probably leave explanation to his reviewers and critics.'[14] When, in spite of such advice, a writer proceeds to characterize a story's heroine, this description suspends the narrative action.[15] The story events stop, though reading or listening may continue.

So here are two approaches to character description: the film that shows countless visual details while the story progresses; the book that selects however many details to assert in between story events. Let's assume, for purposes of comparison, that the same character faces the same dilemma in both of these media. Do children respond any differently to these alternative characterizations? Yes.

Young viewers rely on moving pictures' visual content to understand story characters. Compared to radio[16] and even picture book audiences,[17] children presented fiction on film or TV base more inferences on what characters look like and how they behave. For example, the way an action is performed often suggests its ease or difficulty. Following either a cartoon viewing or picture book reading of *A Story a Story*, I asked children whether hanging the leopard was easy or hard for Ananse. (See the frames in Figures 5.4 to 5.7. He tugs at the rope four times in the film. Only the last picture appears in the book.) The two audiences, cartoon and book, base their inferences on different evidence.[18] Cartoon viewers typically call on observed behavior: 'It was hard,' they will say, because 'it looked like he [Ananse] was struggling' or 'by the way he was pulling the rope.' Picture book audience members more often import evidence from outside the story: 'Hard', because 'leopards are awful heavy' or 'they could bite you.' They also refer to dialogue more often – 'Hard, because the Sky God *said* he was weak' – though listeners and viewers heard identical language.

Like practicing physiognomists, children plumb film and TV characters' appearance for demographic data as well. Costumes help viewers assign fictional characters to a time and place: 'In the old days they wore those kind of clothes' or 'He had wooden shoes, so I know it was [!] Scotland.' (Radio listeners, even hearing a costume described, will resort to more general reasoning: 'It was the olden days, because that's when magic fishes were around.')[19] Beards, breasts and other milestones of maturity

Figure 5.4

Figure 5.5

Figure 5.6

Figure 5.7

offer clues to a character's age: 'He was a young man, because he didn't have a mustache or beard.' Muscles and vigor signal character strength: 'He was weak, because his bones were sticking out' or 'Strong, by the way he carried all those things.'[20] Minute physical details apparent in real life and simulated ever so carefully in production are readily interpreted by young viewers, even though not always correctly.

What about getting to the heart of a fictional character? Assessing personal statistics like age, strength and attractiveness sheds only superficial light on a story's characters. How well do children understand a moving picture hero's or heroine's feelings?

Young children recognize characters' emotions from their facial expressions. By about age six, they reliably identify happy, sad, angry, afraid and surprised-looking faces, though anger and fear are sometimes confused.[21] In fact, younger viewers interpreting a character's feelings tend to rely on the emotions she or he overtly expresses (in facial expression, gesture, posture) and to disregard all other cues, even the situation that induced these feelings.[22] In a sense, film capitalizes on younger children's acceptance of emotions at face value; a single stunning close-up or dramatic gesture is often convincing enough evidence for them. As viewers get older, they learn to base inferences about characters' feelings on many cues, including their outward displays of emotion, possible motives, and the situation they are in. A story's mood or emotional tone is also enhanced by voices, music, sound effects, and the visual effects possible with cameras, lighting and editing. Perhaps the more experienced we become as viewers, the more ingredients contribute to our empathy for film and television characters.

Here is one example of how children interpret on screen characters' emotions. Preschoolers and older nine- and ten-year-olds participated in a study where half the children watched an animated version of the adventure *The Three Robbers*, and the other half were read the picture book on which the film was based.[23] All of the children then were asked how the little girl Tiffany felt about meeting the robbers. (See the film frames in Figures 5.8 to 5.11. A slight variation of the first picture appears in the book.) The narration accompanying both versions is:[24]

> But one bitter, black night the robbers stopped a carriage that had but one passenger, an orphan named Tiffany. She was on her way to live with a wicked aunt. Tiffany was delighted to meet the robbers.

Figure 5.8

Figure 5.9

Figure 5.10

Figure 5.11

The two story audiences tend to reach similar conclusions, but via different routes. Most children who saw the televised cartoon referred to visual evidence in judging Tiffany's feelings. They cited as signs of her fearless response both the faintest hint of a smile – 'She started smiling' – and the presumably friendly gesture of raising a doll to the window – 'She showed one of them her doll.' In contrast, more children hearing the story read aloud called on pertinent text – 'It *said* she was delighted.' Older listeners also drew further inferences – 'She didn't want to go to her aunt's' or 'She didn't know they were robbers.'

One caveat warrants mention. Children tend *not* to volunteer psychological information about story characters. The younger they are, the more children limit their descriptions to characters' actions, dialogue and obvious physical reactions'.[25] Adults who draw children out through conversation can help them to articulate what they know about characters' motives, thoughts and feelings.

Confusions

The camera image   The same verisimilitude that makes moving pictures so legible can also mislead young viewers about what they see. Accepting the screen image too literally confuses children about both objects and events. As a simple example, consider the size an object assumes on a TV screen: when comparing two images of a candy bar videotaped at different distances from the camera, children at second grade level or below tend to see the candy bar in close-up (bigger image) as being more to eat than the one in a medium shot (smaller image).[26] Not until they are older can children be counted on to overlook such apparent differences in image size. Even adult viewers make mistakes sometimes and interpret film content as if there were no intervening camera. For example, they may fail to notice distortions in a shot filmed through a wide angle lens.[27]

Across time and space   A more pervasive confusion among young viewers results from the editing process. What one shows of a story, unless *cinéma-verité*, is not an exhaustive record of events. When film or television fiction is edited, only those segments of a plot judged to best represent the whole story are selected. An editor works to depict just enough information – not so much as to bore viewers or so little as to be frustrating. Joining any two selected pieces of film or videotape transports a story's action instantaneously from one place and time to another, regardless of whether a character moves to another room or another planet. Print and audio media cross similar gaps of space and time in telling a story; book chapters routinely pick up the action: 'Some time later. . . .' But the edited action in film appears continuous:[28]

> Making a smooth cut means joining two shots in such a way that the transition does not create a noticeable jerk and the spectator's illusion of seeing a continuous piece of action is not interrupted.

Film's illusion of uninterrupted narrative action takes a toll on children's sense of time. In several Harvard studies, children ages nine to twelve estimated the duration of story events. Some children witnessed the events on film while others had them described on audiotape or in picture book form. Questions were usually phrased, 'How long did it take Ananse to get up to the Sky God?' or '. . . the flock of geese to travel?' or '. . . the robbers to stop a carriage and rob the passengers?,' followed up by 'How do you know?'

For example, here are the robbers from *The Three Robbers* stopping a carriage to hold up its passengers. The illustrations and text in Figures 5.12 to 5.14 appear in the picture book.

To stop carriages, the robbers blew pepper in the horses' eyes.

Figure 5.12

74

Figure 5.13

Figure 5.14

In the film, pictures are added to animate the characters' villainous actions, as shown in Figures 5.15 to 5.18. The same exact text used in the book is heard on the cartoon's soundtrack.

Figure 5.15

Figure 5.16

Figure 5.17

Figure 5.18

Most cartoon viewers gave the robbers less than five minutes to complete their crime, with some estimates cast in mere seconds. Listeners, even though provided with pictures, extended the job's duration to as long as two hours.[29] In every instance, film viewers ages nine to twelve give shorter time estimates for events than do peers who hear the same events described.[30]

Children's reasoning helps explain their different perceptions. Film spectators defend short estimates of robbing time with reasons like: 'It happened so fast on the screen' or 'It showed them walking pretty fast.' These viewers are confusing the duration of fictional events with the time it takes to present them on screen. As a result, they measure story events in real time. Listeners are more inclined to think through how long narrative actions might actually take. They consider several aspects of the situation being portrayed such as its difficulty – 'It's kind of hard to stop a stagecoach' – and the separate steps involved – 'They have to chop the wheels and all the rest.' Even listeners' shorter estimates suggest a certain pragmatic logic: 'You had to be fast [as a robber]; if not, they would catch you.'

It is as if the film presentation eclipses older children's mastery of time concepts. All these children could tell time and understood words that measure time. That was tested for first. Under other circumstances children this age reason logically about duration.[31] Also witness the listeners' responses. When judging story time in front of the screen, however, many older children attend only to one cue – filmed movement – and therefore make errors in judgment typical of younger children. They succumb to moving pictures' illusion of continuous action across time and space.

We will return after these messages The best of drama on commercial television is frequently interrupted by commercials, as we know all too well. While seeing story action on screen compresses the plot for children, introducing extraneous material makes them lose track of it. Younger children in particular have more trouble relating a character's motives, actions and ensuing consequences when these events are separated in time by advertising. When researchers re-edit a TV episode to reduce this gap – for example, between a protagonist's unworthy motives and violent behavior – the younger viewer better understands how these events relate and can also evaluate the aggressor more negatively.[32] Commercial interruptions are not entirely at fault. Young children's grasp of complex drama is more piecemeal than older audiences', regardless of the medium; they make fewer inferences about the relationships among story events. But these intrusions in television fiction do become a further hindrance to younger viewers' comprehension.

This last example points up something more basic. How well youngsters understand film and television fiction depends on many factors, including whether they can make sense of production techniques such as edited transitions as well as apply general thinking skills and world knowledge. What distinguishes children's learning from the screen, as opposed to other media, is the relative ease with which they attain some level of understanding.

Watching and reading

Does children's exposure to television at home affect their performance at school? Surely the many hours spent in front of the tube are somewhat to blame for declining reading scores. How can they not be?

The answer is not so simple.

For one thing, television's effect on children is hard to measure. The medium so pervades this country's homes that even occasional viewers may see or know enough of television to be affected. And what should we measure? Is the issue how much children watch? – the more watching, the poorer reading? Does it matter what they watch, whether a strict diet of *The Electric Company*'s reading instruction or of action adventure shows? Perhaps the time that children tune in is important; late night viewing may leave students tired for school the next day. One thing seems certain: the relationships reported to exist between children's TV viewing and academic achievement present problems as well as opportunities for education.

Time to practice reading Learning to read takes practice. Since reading words calls for different decoding skills than reading moving pictures, time spent watching TV is time not available to practice reading. True, but television has not taken children away from books. There is no evidence that outside reading activity, except for comic books, has decreased among school children.[33] Even the reduced reading observed when communities first receive television revives once the new medium's novelty wears off.[34] Alas, leisure reading was generally a minor activity for children before television, and it still is.[35] There simply is not much time for TV to erode. This observation should in no way discourage parents from limiting children's viewing or from promoting reading. However, such evidence dispels the notion that instead of watching TV, most children used to spend three to four hours every day reading books.

Moreover, reading and watching are not totally dissimilar mental activities. Some skills needed to understand a story, such as keeping track of successive events, are exercised whether the tale is incised in print, celluloid, or videotape.[36]

Interest in reading Learning to read takes motivation. Children who are aware of books they want to read bring added incentive to the task. Television is often credited with stimulating children to follow up their viewing with related reading.[37] Judging by bookstore sales and library requests, TV and movie-related 'tie-ins' are an important inducement to children and adults alike. But there's one possible problem. While an engaging drama on screen may whet young viewers' appetites for a print version, it may well be a text of lesser literary quality. At particular risk are children who watch considerable television (three or more hours a day) but read very little (less than two books a month). These children

ac   ) at least one study, choose fiction less rich in character
        it, plot and ideas than do other children.[38] I can't help but
        it some of these heavy viewers/infrequent readers are picking
        ovie novelizations to read.[39] These screen spin-offs tend to be
w   ritten and heavily promoted.[40] On one hand, television may
leaa   uctant reader to an inferior book. On the other hand, this may
be a ch. l who, were it not for TV, would be reading comic books. In
either case, television does not appear to be sending children to more
books, but rather to different ones.

Television is unquestionably a potent sales force. The medium is as
capable of generating excitement for classic children's literature as for
second-rate reading. Publishers owe it to children to keep up the literary
standards for moving-picture-related books; they are the informal primers
for many young readers in America today.

Family support for reading   Learning to read takes effort and ability. The
help families provide to young children learning to read probably has
more bearing on their reading achievement than does how much
television they watch. Many studies do show that children who watch
more TV do less well in reading, but by itself this is misleading
information. For one thing, to say that television watching and reading
achievement are related does not necessarily imply that watching affects
achievement. Perhaps it works the other way; because a child is a less
competent reader, he or she chooses television over books as an activity.
Even more likely, both viewing habits and reading performance may be
products of some other factors. When researchers compare children of
similar intelligence and social class, the negative relationship between
viewing and reading becomes less significant.[41] For primary grade
students in particular, family income, parents' approach to media and
children's attitudes toward reading are found to better predict reading
achievement than how much television is watched.[42] Third graders with
higher reading scores have parents who value reading and make print
materials available. The students themselves think of reading as a source
of pleasure and learning.

A home environment that encourages and enhances reading activities
helps children succeed at reading. Conversely, a family that ignores print
and stresses television as the primary entertainer, teacher and compan-
ion, may impede their children's reading development.

Television should not be incriminated as the enemy of children's
education. I am not the first one to say: it is not the medium itself, but

how it is used that determines its value to people. Television offers children more ready access to fiction than perhaps any medium ever has. Movies do too, but children have to leave home and pay to see them. As we reviewed, even young children eyeing the screen can apprehend a story's central action and characters' reactions to what is happening. The educational challenge here is not so much helping children to make sense of the given. It is teaching them to relate what they have seen and heard on TV to the world beyond the screen. It is reminding them of what is figure and what is ground.

Hands on

There are so many possible ways to enrich children's television experiences. Every parent and teacher responsible for children needs to decide what, if any, intervention is called for. Children enjoy watching television. Some of us may simply prefer to permit them their entertainment. At the other extreme are advocates of formal curricula designed to make children into critical, TV-literate young viewers. In between is a position where adults can use television stories and movies to teach, learn from, and just have fun with their children.

Watching together

Just joining children for a TV program or movie can enhance the quality of their attention. Perhaps in their eyes your presence increases the legitimacy of what they are doing and makes them regard it more seriously. They may also feel good about having you there. From the adult's pespective, sitting in informs you about what your children are seeing and hearing, about what kinds of characters and fantasies they are witnessing.

Screen talk   Children's comprehension also benefits when adults make the effort to clarify or interpret moving picture content for them, such as explaining an event's importance, or pointing out its relationship to earlier events. Even though conversation cannot flow as freely as when you narrate a story, there is time both during and following a TV episode or movie to share your reactions and hear theirs. In the process of exchange, you discover what about a given plot stands out for them. Furthermore, you have the opportunity to inject your own feelings and values or to correct their misconceptions.

(1) Are children engaged by a character's dilemma for example? Ask them if they would do what the character did and why.

(2) See if they appreciate a character's motives: ask why did he or she do that?

(3) Explore children's judgments of character actions: ask, do you think what he or she did was a good idea, a bad idea, or what?

(4) Also review suggestions for discussing stories in chapter 3, Hands On.

Playing games with a VCR   The video cassette recorder is a marvelous piece of equipment to play story games with. Endless guessing games can be invented by stopping and restarting a story at different points.

(1) Stop a cassette featuring a mystery long enough to have each viewer predict who committed the crime, where the jewels are hidden etc., and give the evidence for their prediction.

(2) An action-adventure episode can be interrupted to speculate about what will happen next – how will the hero escape from harm or the heroine outwit the villain?

(3) A well-liked story could be reviewed more than once. Each time have children look or listen for something else.

(4) Scrutinize production techniques too: see who notices the most scene changes or special visual effects.

It may seem frustrating to stop the dramatic action in mid-course. Then again, most American children have been dealing with commercial interruptions all their lives.

Producing something new

Television and movies can be very provocative for young viewers. Why not let children put their energy to creative use.

(1) Writing television and movie reviews
- Why limit children to book reviews? Children also can submit their experiences with TV and movies to written review. In addition, the exercise will make them more aware of what goes into a complex

production.

- First devote some time to discussing what information about a TV show or movie needs to be included in a review. To do justice to these audiovisual media, comments may be called for about such elements as the soundtrack, scenery, costumes and acting.

- If a book version exists, some children could review a story in print, others from the screen; then they can compare notes.

(2) Staging dramas
- Have children write short scripts in the style of popular TV shows or movies: for example, soap operas, situation comedies, superhero adventures, or science fiction. Different children will need to be responsible for acting, costumes, lighting, music, etc., depending on how simple or elaborate a production you all decide to mount.

- Those interested in commercials can develop new products, make models of their packaging, and try selling them to classmates or friends.

- The audience votes on which of the products promoted they would most or least want to buy.

- Have someone videotape children's performance so they can see themselves on screen. Sometimes schools have video equipment and a faculty person who can instruct motivated students in using a camera. Some community cable TV services offer the public access to video equipment and studio facilities.

(3) Try pantomime
- Each individual or group plans a very short story to act out using gesture, facial expression and body movement. No speaking is allowed, but perhaps sound effects and props are permitted.

- Adapt the rules to children's abilities.

- Spectators try and retell in words what they think went on.

- Show a mime film to prepare children.

If your own motivation flags, remember: children who invest more in their viewing get more out of it.

Chapter 6

Does television stifle imagination?

It seems obvious: seeing a story on television imposes on the viewer someone else's vision. Youngsters' perceptions of a narrative are supplied by a Hanna-Barbera animation studio or a producer like Norman Lear. Listening and reading, on the other hand, leave audience members free to imagine for themselves how a story looks. As one nine-year-old explained: 'when you listen to a story, you get to make all the pictures in your mind.' And even as an adult, haven't you experienced the discrepancy between your impression of a novel's characters and their subsequent appearance in a television or film adaptation? 'Why, in my picture of the hero he has no mustache, and the heroine is much too tall and pretty. What poor casting!' Surely television suppresses children's exercise of imagination, whereas radio and print encourage it. TV is made the culprit again.

This is logical but short-sighted reasoning. It overlooks where our imagery comes from. To imagine means to make a picture or image in your mind. Try it.

Imagine a fish

See this fish in your mind's eye as clearly as you can. It may help to close your eyes for a moment. How did you know to picture it this way? What sources did you consult? Perhaps you remembered fish you bought at the store or caught at the seashore? Or maybe you thought of fish you once kept in a tank or saw in a picture? Adult and child alike, we all accumulate mental notes about the world around us which we plumb on such occasions. These surroundings include art images – pictures from product packages, billboards, buses, books, magazines, movies, television, video games and fine art as well.

Does watching television inhibit children from generating their own visual images and limit development of their imaginations? Does viewing fiction add anything to children's creative resources? Let's look closely at how children's image-making process is actually affected by seeing stories on television.

Choosing tasks to use with children

Telling about television Children telling about a TV episode rarely offer visual description of its settings, characters, or props. There are exceptions; a powerful car, extreme haircut, occasionally even a special visual effect will particularly interest them and be described in considerable detail. For the most part, however, children say little about what scenery looks like or what characters are wearing – let alone how things on screen are lighted, positioned and filmed.

Why don't children account for a television story's appearance more fully? If video displays are so compelling for young viewers, why don't we hear more about costume changes, camera angles and close-ups? We know that children rely on pictures to recall and interpret a story and that their choice of illustration may even be based on a picture's formal features. It therefore seems unlikely that they fail to notice or quickly forget what story content looks like.

There are several possible explanations. One concerns the production side of television. Earlier I pointed out the dilemma of detecting listeners' awareness of sounds or music that are meant to add unobtrusively to a story's overall effect. Likewise, the innumerable visual details of setting, costumes, lights, camera angles, editing, etc., are composed so that no one element stands out. Once engrossed in a TV drama, even astute adults have a difficult time sustaining their attention to such technical aspects of production. Try it.

Furthermore, we are dealing with young audiences. The more youthful the eye, the less knowledgeable children are about production, and the more inclined they are to look 'through' the pictures for meaningful content. While older children are better equipped to tease out a story's formal features, they are not necessarily trained to do so. Young viewers are not often encouraged to wax eloquent about a screen adventure's special visual effects or, for that matter, taught the vocabulary needed to describe such craft. This information is not essential to convey a story's plot or main points; it is beside the point. Nonetheless, without all the staging and special effects, there would be no point portrayed.

Children's sparse accounts of TV fiction's appearance have another, more basic explanation. Children asked to talk or write about what they have seen on television must translate picture information into words. Video content is easy enough to observe, but it cannot be exhaustively described. Meaning also is changed and lost when one set of symbols is used to explain another. In comparison, verbal story content like dialogue needs only to be repeated. Interestingly, students' writing styles show signs of being affected by their television viewing. When narratives of third, fifth and eighth graders were analyzed, those stories composed by heavy prime-time viewers read more like screenplays than prose: they used fewer words per sentence, filled in fewer gaps in the flow of time, and reminded adult readers of watching action take place from afar.[1]

Getting closer to visual imagery For children to reveal more of what they see on television, they need to report their observations using materials and methods that share important features with those of video images.[2] What children remember of television imagery is tapped most directly by having them produce like images with film and video cameras, animation, and computer graphics. Admittedly, these activities entail investments of time, money and expert supervision.[3] And even those youngsters who achieve some mastery of these formats will still have a hard job recreating the sophistication of most American TV production. But no matter how challenging, these are the means of expression fully equipped to express children's visual experiences with television and movies.

Simpler methods also can be used to advantage. As traditional a task as having children draw after a story can be surprisingly revealing. Children making pictures can readily display all kinds of information they notice on the screen yet tend not to mention: shapes of objects; characters' stature, facial features and dress; scenery; spatial relationships among characters and props in a setting; etc. Strictly speaking, drawing is best suited to represent visual information about animation as opposed to live action. Though all manner of things can be animated, from puppets to sand, most televised cartoons consist of successive drawings. Conversely, we would expect the effect of watching cartoons to show up in the graphic artwork children do.

Yet using children's drawings as a measure of their imagination or visual memory has serious limitations. We cannot equate children's pictures with their mental imagery.[4] For one thing, children notice and may remember features that they don't include in their own artwork: how thick or thin lines are, how shading is done, and the mood a drawing conveys may be perceived by first graders but not displayed in their pictures for several more years.[5] How children like an object to be drawn also may differ from the way they depict it themselves: a third grader may draw a house from the front, yet prefer to see one drawn in conventional perspective.[6] It's hard to say which picture is closer to his or her internal image.

Drawing skill is an obvious issue, as children vary widely in their ability to draw what they imagine. It is common to see a grade school student crumple up several attempts at a drawing, complaining that he or she just can't get it right. If no model is present, youngsters are likely measuring their work against an imagined standard of reference and finding their version wanting. Their critical abilities tend to be more advanced than their productive abilities.

A child's intention is another factor. Preschoolers approach drawing in a playful, experimental way. At this age, children often have only a very general goal in mind when they pick up a marker. Four-year-olds who decide to draw a person may record in figural form some of their subject's characteristics – a shape for the head, one for the body, lines for the arms and legs – but they feel no obligation to conform to standards of realism or other established conventions.[7] The largest figure on the paper may be the most important one to them rather than the one actually of greatest size. In contrast, once children reach age seven or eight, they become interested if not preoccupied with drafting a world in as realistic and literal a manner as possible.[8] It is these school-age children who presumably will try harder to recreate in recognizable forms whatever television material haunts their memories.

How structured a given drawing task is also affects the final product. Young children will produce one version of the human figure in a free drawing and another one in a figure completion task.[9]

Mental images are elusive. The very act of realizing them in any tangible form changes them. The challenge which artists of all ages face is to express their personal image in some equivalent form suitable to the medium in which they are working.[10] Lines, dots and contours not given in nature must be used to express the graphic artist's vision. Even skilled artists report differences between their original idea and the finished piece.[11] Studying children's drawings cannot tell us how they see things in their mind's eye. Drawing is not even a graphic translation of all a child knows about his or her subject. It always implies selection and interpretation. But drawings do give us an inkling of the content of a remembered visual image. They are similar in important respects to the television children watch, and in particular to cartoons, which already are converted into lines, dots and contours. Moreover, drawing is accesible to children as a form of visual expression. Individual styles of drawing are detected in children's pictures as early as age five.[12] And our main concern in this chapter is with the effects of highly visual media on children's own creative output.

Other methods of tapping children's visual imagery for stories can supplement or substitute for drawing. One way to compensate for limited drawing skill is to let children describe discrepancies between their picture and their imagined rendering of a scene. What needs to be added, omitted, or changed? Conversation about story appearance is often more vivid with a picture there as a starting point. Instead of producing their own story graphics, children can arrange figures to show where characters are or how scenery and props are arranged. Something as simple as a piece of square white paper can stand for floor or ground, and cut-out shapes may represent different characters. In the Hands On section, I will return to suggestions for activities.

The point is: not only does the medium in which we tell a story bias the content it delivers. The tests we give a young audience also bias what they can tell us about a story. After children watch television fiction, we should attend to what they can show us, not only to what they can say.

Picturing the pictures

How does seeing a story animated affect children's drawings? Let's look at what nine- and ten-year-olds drew after screening a cartoon of the Grimms' fairy tale, *The Fisherman and His Wife*.[13] As you may know, the poor fisherman in this tale repeatedly summons a magic fish he has caught and relays to it his wife's ever greater demands.

The fisherman fishing   For one drawing, each viewing child was asked to 'think about the fisherman fishing until you can see him doing that in your mind. Now draw the fisherman, as best you can, the way you see it in your mind.'[14] The cartoon audience heard this narration:

Each morning he went down to the shore and cast his net for fish.

They also saw him cast his net a total of four times during the story. Other children, assigned instead to listen to an audio recording of the story, heard the following description of the film action:

Each morning he went down to the shore and lifted his net high above his head and flung it out over the sea where it gently floated down for fish.

Reference to him casting his net was made three more times. A third, baseline group of students had no exposure to the fairy tale, but drew pictures of 'a fisherman fishing.' These baseline drawings provide us with some examples of how children this age depict subject matter like that in the story. Alll children had up to five minutes to complete a pencil sketch.

The drawings in Figures 6.1 to 6.6 were done as baseline, by listeners, and by cartoon viewers. The last drawing is a traced film frame. As you might predict, the film viewers' pictures resemble the screen image, whereas the listeners depict more varied scenes. But even more striking is the extent to which the listeners' renderings contradict the story text: in half of their drawings, the fisherman was shown with a fishing pole, while all but one film viewer had him use a net. Listening children disregarded information given four times in the audio story. It isn't that they didn't hear the narrator's description; most children could pick it out among several alternative phrasings. The baseline drawings offer a clue. Many of these young New Englanders picture a man with rod and reel as their prototype fisherman at work, with the traditional beard, boots, hat and pail. Some listeners apparently hold on to that image despite the text; they refer more often than viewers to sources for their imagery outside the story, including people they have seen fishing, times they have gone fishing, even illustrations they remember from books. Listeners' images are indeed based more on their personal experience, but they also are more limited by it.

The wife's last wish   Here the film and listening audiences were

Figure 6.2 Listener

Figure 6.1 Baseline

Figure 6.3 Listener

Figure 6.4 Viewer

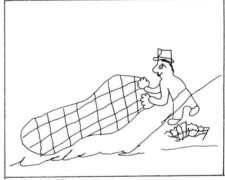

Figure 6.5 Viewer

Figure 6.6 Film frame

reminded of the point, later in the story, when the fisherman's wife wakes up her husband and demands to be ruler of the universe: in her words, 'I wish to be like unto God.' Children were asked to 'draw the way the wife looks to you when she tells her husband that last wish.' The listening audience heard her facial expression described literally:

> She turned to him and opened her mouth wide, showing her big white teeth. Her eyebrows turned down and she said. . . .

Film viewers saw her face in close-up as she spoke. An intense moment in both versions, the greedy wife raises her voice and makes her demand against a clash of cymbals. Children providing baseline pictures were instructed: 'Draw a woman who has everything in the world she wants and is demanding she be given one more thing.'

In Figures 6.7 to 6.12 are several wife drawings done as baseline, by listeners, and by cartoon viewers. Last is a tracing of a film frame. What, if any, emotion do these drawings convey? According to adult raters, film viewers were least likely to portray the wife with a happy, smiling face. Instead most young viewers rendered a recognizably angry face (as in 6.10) or one with an ambiguous expression (as in 6.11). These latter drawings seem like less successful attempts to produce a figure like the angry one in the film. In fact, most film viewers thought the wife was angry and based their opinion on how she appeared the moment she made the wish: 'I could tell by the mean way she looked at him.'

A single film or video image can supply children with compelling, memorable evidence about a character's feelings.

In comparison, children who heard the story recording roamed the plot for information about her emotions. Most of them decided the wife felt happy when she made her last wish: 'well, she had everything, a castle, a husband, she could rule the weather, a black dress . . .' and failed to take into account that she still was not satisfied. Likewise, the listeners showed less of the drama associated with making an outrageous demand, picturing instead the smiling female typical of baseline sketches.

Cartoon viewers' pictures also differed from the others' in their scale. More nine- and ten-year-olds who saw the story animated drew the wife's face in 'close-up' as opposed to the full figure favored by listeners and baseline providers.

The magic fish Remember the fish you conjured up earlier? Now try to make it look like a magic fish coming up out of the water, and you have a

Figure 6.8 Listener

Figure 6.7 Baseline

Figure 6.9 Listener

Figure 6.10 Viewer

Figure 6.12 Film frame

Figure 6.11 Viewer

baseline image for the last example. In the story the fisherman summons the fish four times on behalf of his wife: 'Flounder, flounder in the sea, Come, I pray thee, here to me. . . .' After each meeting the fish sends the man home. The children were instructed to 'think about the last time the fish said "Go home" ' and to 'draw the fish then, the way you see it in your mind.' Listeners heard the following description of the fish before it spoke:

> A shimmering golden glow surrounded the fish as his face peered out of the water.

Film viewers saw this shot of the fish on four occasions.

One again, we can see in the drawings in Figures 6.13 to 6.18 the cartoon's impact on its audience. Only students who saw the fish facing front as it rose from the water tried recreating this image. Judging by the baseline drawings, such a view is indeed unusual; youngsters providing baseline pictures never drew the fish from the front. Nor did any listeners: it is difficult to specify in words the point of view from which a character should be imagined every time it appears, and questionable whether such description can change the way listeners like to picture a character themselves.

The orientation most commonly used when drawing a fish is a profile. (Oddly, no one – not even the filmmaker – correctly pictured the flounder as a flat fish with eyes at the top of its head.) Most children and adults draw the orientation that lets them define an object's visual features the simplest way in two dimensions.[15] Children prefer drawing men and houses from the front, for example, but horses and cars from the side.[16] Drawing a fish in profile is a perfectly adequate solution and permits a young artist to include a good deal of fishy information.

Nevertheless, seeing a cartoon depict a character in an atypical view encouraged some children to do the same in their own artwork. And it is just this kind of uncommon approach to a graphic problem that identifies some children as being more original and creative.[17]

Summing up

In summing up, it is borne out that listening to fiction can rouse children's imaginative juices. Few nine- and ten-year-old listeners asked had trouble imagining how they wanted the tale's characters, props and setting to look. Moreover, the listening audience has to infer the pictures

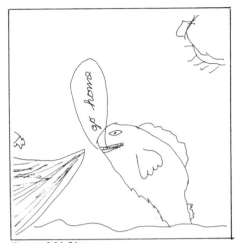

Figure 6.14 Listener

Figure 6.13 Baseline

Figure 6.15 Listener

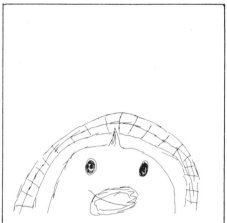

Figure 6.17 Viewer

Figure 6.16 Viewer

Figure 6.18 Film frame

it conjures up, basing these inferences largely on remembered experiences with similar people, objects and places. Granted, words vary in their power to evoke vivid mental pictures and the descriptive language in this story may have been too brief and subtle to suggest images to children. More explicit text – 'The wife was furious; she fell into a rage'[18] – might boost children's production of angry-looking women. So might more dramatic use of sound effects and music. Even then, the absence of pictures still permits children considerable license to interpret a story visually. To this extent, hearing or reading a story without illustration encourages children's exercise of imagination.

But the degree to which children visualize a narrative they hear also must vary. This study's tasks prompted children to generate story images after the fact. We don't know how much visualizing children do on their own while they listen. Other senses, such as touch and taste, may be more easily aroused by words than sight.[19]

And even when imaging does occur among young listeners, it is actually limited by their prior experience with a story's content. Radio stories set in remote places may entice an audience to invent their own scenery, borrowing bits and pieces from more familiar sites, or they may just elicit vague mental pictures. Nor do listening children always avail themselves of the images implied by a story text; as we have seen, youngsters accustomed to having men fish out of boats with poles may prefer picturing them that way, regardless of descriptions to the contrary.

Television, on the other hand, supplies ready-made images, which young viewers do use as models for their own story pictures. We have seen nine- and ten-year-olds trying to reproduce in their sketches cartoon features ranging from details of setting and facial expression to the orientation of figures in space.

Children's attempts to picture what they have seen in cartoons may be glibly dismissed as imitative: 'They saw the wife's face look a certain way and that's what they drew. So what?' Critics can conceivably raise skeptical eyebrows any time young viewers' behavior recapitulates video and film images, including when they re-enact TV adventures in their make-believe play[20] or use video content to solve problems creatively.[21]

But such a negative interpretation fails to take other evidence into account. Imagination can only use what memory has to offer.[22] Most school age children exhibit prescribed ways of drawing people, situating them in space, making them happy, etc., as noted in their baseline drawings. Access to a single animated story stimulated children to stretch their schemes and try doing something different. Children's artwork benefits as well when they draw directly from a model rather than from memory; drawing from observation helps a youngster study a model closely and capture more information about its physical features on paper.[23] The most ready aids to young artists may be those illustrations, comics, TV and film images already reduced to two dimensions; they are simpler and more abstract than the real objects to which they refer.[24] Models do not have to be the stimulus for slavish copying.[25] Memorable animation can also inspire children to express themselves graphically in new ways, even to see things anew.

If some research does find television stunting viewers' imaginative thinking – there is no persuasive evidence right now – it will not be due to any fault inherent in the medium. Rather, it will be because children watch too much of too little. Children's TV programs don't always exploit their physical resources; fantasy characters in cartoons could move and change appearance in the most marvelous ways, but in practice often just move their mouths.[26] Nor are youngsters always encouraged to make use of the repertoire of media images they do see. Creative ability develops only when children practice expressing their imagination; seeing is not enough.

Video is the dominant source of images in today's culture and a critical ingredient in most American children's visual education. We could feed children's imaginations by upgrading the quality and diversity of the television they watch and by helping them use viewing experiences in the interest of their own personal expression.

Hands on

Art education in perspective

Teaching children art has meant different things to educators over the years. At one extreme have been teachers who trained their students to painstakingly render objects directly from a model. At the other have been those who protected young people's fertile imaginations from any such intervention, leaving them to blossom on their own. Neither approach seems totally satisfying. Perhaps that is one reason why the pendulum in art education has swung back and forth, emphasizing first one, then the other strategy.

There is a time for children to observe the external world and a time to honor their inner dreams. Observing real people, objects and surroundings informs children's memory, whereas imaginative exercises let them explore what they already know.

There is a time for children to experience media images and a time to learn things firsthand. Art, literature, movies, and television offer children access to someone else's insight and sense of a thing, while seeing the world directly leaves the selecting and interpreting to them.

There is a time for children to reuse a material, tool, or technique, and a time to try something new. Copying their own prior efforts allows young artists opportunities to practice and refine their skills, whereas experimenting may result in new discoveries.

The trick is to help children strike a happy balance among these factors, according to their current needs and inclinations. This may take some experimenting on your part. Always look for a child's personality in his or her creative work. Remember, the greatest artists are those who have found a suitable medium and style in which to express their personal reactions to experience.

Strengthening children's imagery

Children can imagine a thing in its absence from a very tender age. The baby who searches for a ball that has rolled behind a chair is acknowledging her belief that it exists even though she can no longer see it. Working at optimum efficiency, a child imagines a given item easily, vividly, in diverse, even original ways. To help children strengthen and stretch this ability, teach them to notice their surroundings with all their senses and to represent their experience in as many forms as they can.

Suggestions for exercising visual imagery

(1) Imagining variations on a theme
- Begin by having children pick a favorite animal and imagine it to themselves without telling you its name.
- Have them describe it as fully as possible until you can guess what it is. If you need more information, ask about its size, color, legs, wings, fins, tail, etc.
- Then ask them to imagine and describe their animal – say it's a fish – doing something it loves to do (swim) or something it hates doing (dangle on a hook, sit in a whale's belly).
- Let them experiment with scene changes. Where would they find their animal (fish tank)? Hide their animal (coral reef, fish wallpaper)? Play

with it (bathtub, puddle)? Put it to bed (on ice cubes)?

- Try the same exercise using inanimate objects.

(2)   Drawing from memory
- Have children invent or choose an imaginary creature to draw. To help children expand on their pictures, ask questions like: What does it want to do next? Who is its enemy? its friend? What do its mother and father look like? What special powers does it have? Does it ever dress up?
- Have children depict a real animal or person doing something impossible or fantastic. They may want to draw some of the scenes they imagined in (1).
- Ask children to draw some familiar object or scene. Use a simple toy or item for younger ones. Older ones could make a picture or map of their classroom, bedroom, or favorite store. Compare across children and against the actual location.

(3)   Drawing from observation (for older children)
- Select an object that interests your children, perhaps a pair of sneakers, a bicycle, or toy.
- Tell children to look carefully at the subject while they draw and to follow its contour with their pencil or marker.
- Remove object and finished drawing. Let children try drawing it again from memory, first right away, the next time after an hour, then after a day.
- Completed drawings may be compared against the object and revised.

Try point of view drawings too:
- Have a group of children sit around a table.
- Place the object to be drawn in the middle.
- Ask each child to try depicting the object from his or her point of view.
- When everyone is finished, look at the drawings in order. See if the object begins to rotate.

(4)   Modeling the media
- Let children select a picture to draw from comic books, magazines, record album covers, or books.
- Encourage them to reproduce as many details in their picture as they like, but discourage tracing.

- They also may change the original in their version to make it funnier, more mysterious, etc.
- Use film and television show screenings as the stimulus for art activities. Consider matching the art materials to those used on screen: follow up live action with a photography session, clay animation with clay modeling, a drawn cartoon with drawing or painting.

(5)   Drawing in sequence
- Have children tell a story in a series of pictures. You might give them a set number of empty frames or leave the length up to them.
- If single frames are done on index cards, have the creator of each story sequence shuffle the cards, give them to someone else, and have the new person put the cards in an order that makes sense.

Make flip books:
- Give each child a small pad of unlined paper.
- Explain how the illusion of movement is achieved by changing the position of an object very gradually from one page to the next.
- Begin on the last page. Have children trace this picture, with slight variations, on the page before.
- Have children try a simple movement like raising a dog's tail and ears, or having a rocket lift up and explode off the page.

Chapter 7

Choosing heroes and heroines

When a child loves a story, chances are, he or she has found a sympathetic character to admire and enjoy. An alluring story is one that offers children someone appealing doing something interesting; it could be comic Curious George disobeying directions, it could be daring Indiana Jones fighting off a hundred venomous snakes. Fiction speaks to children through its characters. The meaning youngsters derive from a story – the slant they assume toward a narrative's circumstances and the emotions a story evokes in them – depends on the characters they care about. Curious George makes mistakes that can be laughed at, Indiana Jones exhibits courage and good fortune that can be counted on. Chosen characters, in turn, serve as models for children's developing values. By their appearance, actions, personality and moral fiber, well-liked characters suggest standards for children to adopt or aspire after. To fully appreciate the place of any medium's storytelling in children's lives requires knowing who their fictional heroes and heroines are, and just what about these characters has, however briefly, captured their hearts and imaginations.

102

Who qualifies as a fictional hero and heroine

'. . . first and foremost the hero is one who is willing to set out, take the first step, shoulder something. He is ready to answer for his life . . . and put himself at the service of whatever necessity arises.'[1]

To this role, we most readily assign characters who possess superior bravery, brains, brawn, or other admirable traits. Their powers or abilities exceed ours, their actions are marvelous. These traditional heroes function within the fantastic worlds of fairy tales and myths, where they are either born divine or aided in their quest by some form of magic: a potion they may drink or eat, an object they may purchase, a creature who places itself at their disposal, granting wishes or making promises . . . 'Sometime I'll be of use to you.'[2] For such bigger-than-life characters, the ordinary constraints of nature and society are irrelevant or at least slightly suspended. They hover seductively somewhere above the law.

Heroine status in these genres is conferred without the same exertion of effort. A heroine's actions tend to be more limited than her male counterpart's. In most fairy tales, she is the prize rather than the prize winner, the object of a sentence more often than its subject.

But this narrow view of heroes and heroines excludes many worthy candidates. Isn't the emergence of some hero or heroine a universal feature of fiction? To broaden our definition requires that we acknowledge characters whose power to act is more like our own.[3] Without heroes subject to the laws of nature, society, and to frailties of the human heart and mind, there would be no realistic fiction, nor any tragedy or comedy. The perils they face are often less grave, their victories thus more mundane. But vulnerable heroines and heroes can arouse giggles, sympathy, and even admiration, coping with everyday problems. Think of Lucille Ball's unpredictable maneuvers on *I Love Lucy* or the elegant pathos of a penniless Charlie Chaplin. We comfort ourselves with what in us corresponds to the hero or heroine. In more plausible characters, we find friendlier, more reassuring company.

Our lowering the threshold for hero status is crucial for understanding the full range of children's character preferences. From their less powerful, less experienced vantage point, more resources and activities are out of reach, and therefore become a potential source of fantasies. Character behavior which may be far from impressive to us commands many children's interest and respect: consider the protagonist who drives a fast car or one who decides her own bedtime. To a preadolescent, needing a shave or applying makeup can seem romantic instead of routine.

New media, same old heroes To appreciate the continuity across generations in children's heroes and heroines, such as similarities between your childhood favorites and your children's, it will help to look through characters' superficial appearance to their personality and approach to situations. Try and undress them mentally. For, apart from a few tenacious classics, most of the characters to whom youngsters relate progress out of print as quickly as they entered it. But beneath the transience, certain generic traits continue to resurface in each generation, with updated props, costumes and sets. The maverick hero still rides into a town plagued with villains. He has just upgraded his horsepower from a palomino stallion to a turbo engine. The superhero has bionic powers now, and no longer need rely on the gods for favors. The source of a romantic hero's power is electronic. Because literature and media are both cultural products, their use of specific character types and fictional themes does shift somewhat with the political and social spirit of the time.[4] As one likely consequence of the Women's Movement, there are cropping up more and more female protagonists capable of independent action. (I don't mean witches or fairies, either.) Nonetheless, pivotal character actions tend to be repeated: struggle and victory, pursuit and deliverance, prohibition and violation. As conventional a heroine as Snow White violated the dwarfs' warning not to let in strangers, just as years later spunky Peter Rabbit disregarded his mother's prohibition against entering Mr McGregor's garden. And we all know how much trouble that caused.

It is not that children's fiction simply repeats itself – it evolves along with our knowledge of literature, illustration and life – but rather that stories continue to address wishes, feelings and ideas which recur in all youthful human beings.

Why fiction is so important a source of heroes and heroines

Fiction in any medium is a 'two-headed' experience. There is what the text offers, whether in words, pictures, or performance, and there is what the audience brings to the text. In the words of the novelist Laurence Sterne: 'The truest respect which you can pay to the reader's understanding is to halve this matter amicably, and leave him something to imagine, in his turn, as well as yourself.'[5]

To the story maker falls the job of creating a 'secondary world,'[6] which resembles the real world in varying degrees. Within this imagined universe, what the author, illustrator, or producer relates is 'true;' it conforms with the laws of that world. When a story maker's art is good enough, audience members can 'enter' and be persuaded by this other world. While inside, they imaginatively experience the action and act out different roles. Listeners, readers, viewers, all construct their interpretation of the story, their text within the text.[7]

As intensely as we may experience a story, it still remains safe. No action is required for us to participate, save whatever page turning or other movements are needed to make the fiction accessible. Dangerous missions can be carried out, painful losses endured, the happiest endings savored – all without risk in the real world. And yet the story is 'happening' to its characters, especially to the hero or heroine singled out. Maybe, just maybe, someday, it could happen for the spectator too. That sense of possibility and our power to embrace or dismiss it at will makes fiction a valuable playground, where we can try out our personal fantasies and even extensions to our own personalities.

Children are more prepared than adults to believe their fantasies may come true. And their fantasies encompass a much wider range. Such openness greatly increases the potential influence of a story. But it also means that children will try to keep threatening events at a greater distance; simply casting animals as main characters allows a child to explore difficult problems more comfortably. It is revealing that when children put unacceptable actions in their own compositions, they tend to set the tales in unrealistic places and past times, leaving themselves out of the trouble they invent.[8]

Children's criteria for heroines and heroes

Children are practicing, albeit more playfully than most adults, to be heroines and heroes of their own life stories. As they get older, they become more and more curious about what kinds of looks, behavior, possessions and personalities are desirable to cultivate. Their information sources go beyond family, school and church – the traditional child trainers. The people whose opinions children respect, the ones they will strive to be like, now include some they only meet in the media. And the self-contained, focused portrayals in fiction are more neatly packaged – and in a way easier to grasp – than the complex, ongoing performance of a parent or teacher. Moreover, fictional characters are by nature engaging, and, unlike parents, are never critical of children's behavior.

In their choice of heroes and heroines, children disclose their interests, problems and hopes. This is especially true of characters and stories they seek out again and again. Youngsters learn more about these chosen characters than about other, less favored figures.[9] They invest more feelings in their heroes' plotted failures and triumphs. When children find a character who in their eyes has appealing qualities, they are also saying something about themselves.

Younger children Young children choose as heroes and heroines characters who have play value, whose adventures they can simulate, no matter how extraordinary.

Boys are fascinated by the remarkable physical abilities and strength of superheroes.[10] If they were, say, Superman, then they too 'could fly and break walls, even break a house' – truly a staggering prospect! Admittedly a wishful identification, young boys still stretch to find real similarities between themselves and such fantastic characters, such as a common hair cut, shirt color, or gender. The boundaries of reality blur a little in the wake of their personal fantasies.

Young girls' occupation with physical traits leans more toward concerns with attractiveness. Still. Ideal heroines are described as both pretty and personable.[11] A yet more traditional bent is reflected in sales figures for doll clothes. Some years back, the Mattel Company, which makes the popular Barbie doll, offered such workaday costumes for her as a doctor's outfit and an astronaut's jumpsuit. It seems that these items didn't sell well, though; girls persist in outfitting this glamorous doll in formfitting gowns, jewels and furs. And thanks to Barbie's clothes-consciousness, Mattel professes to be the largest manufacturer of female clothing in the world.[12]

Yet little girls also are intrigued by the notoriously ugly witch, though more hesitant about trading places. Perhaps their interest in such an opposite, unattractive extreme derives from these characters' access to power: the prototype princess, though irresistible in other ways, often lacks it, whereas the witch mercilessly wields it. The desire to exercise control over their own actions also may help explain why young girls sometimes choose male characters with whom to identify.[13] A head count of protagonists in young children's fiction probably would still reveal more males than females; when girls want to assume a leading role in some fictive adventure, there are likely more interesting male parts available to choose from.

Girls' crossing over sex to choose characters illustrates a general flexibility in young children's selection of heroes and heroines. More than older audiences, young girls and boys are willing to adopt as models characters in other than human guises, such as animals, machines and puppets. Think of the mechanical heroes of the 1940s, *Little Toot* (a tugboat) and the *Little Engine That Could* (a train), or the more recent robotic favorites, R2D2 and C3PO, from the *Star Wars* trilogy. Think of the winning young visitor to movie theaters from another planet, *ET*. Less tied to realism, more tempted by anthropomorphism, young children are freer to find a fictional ally in almost any form. It's a character's plight and way of coping that is ultimately meaningful to children.[14]

Older children With age, children distinguish more clearly between characters they wish to be like and those they actually resemble. One sixth grader humbly acknowledged his greater similarity to a realistic TV character than to a superhero, explaining: 'Because, like, he's a normal guy and I'm no special guy.'[15] Older children still sometimes favor bigger-than-life heroes and heroines; but they have a firmer, more adult grip on how implausible, or totally fantastic, an appealing character can be.

As one result of their more pragmatic thinking, older boys and girls often seek out same-sex human characters in their own age range. A preadolescent's interest in more realistic protagonists goes along with an appetite for social information. For twelve-year-olds eager to be popular, realistic fiction offers a useful, no-risk reference for everyday life or for situations being anticipated in the future: think of the down-to-earth dilemmas faced by young characters in Judy Blume's novels or those caricatured on situation comedies. Even the choice of what book to read or TV program to watch becomes more subject to peer review.

Note the parallel between what interests different-aged children about a character and the kind of mental work they do to understand his or her portrayal. Younger boys and girls follow a story's discrete character actions – especially the more vivid, visible ones – and find appealing highly recognizable, idealized protagonists. In comparison, older youngsters make broader, better integrated inferences about characters' roles and personalities and likewise appreciate stories with more complex social messages and models.

At its core, children's choice of heroes and heroines results from the combined vote of their intellect and feelings. That children find a given story more or less realistic is less important than whether they perceive it to be relevant to their lives.[16] Children just measure relevance differently at different ages. One eleven-year-old girl summed up her attitude toward fiction this way: 'You realize things in stories. Even though they are fictional, there are meanings that are real inside the story.'[17]

Theoretically, there are as many heroines and heroes as there are facets to children's personalities. Ideally, we would have at the ready the right character for the right moment and emotion in a child's life: a comic hero when children are feeling inadequate, a character who overcomes a scary predicament when they are coping with some fear, a romantic adventurer when children are testing their own independence. I say 'theoretically' because young audiences experience only a finite number of the characters available, who, in turn, are preselected by the media which present them.

The special – and not so special – case of television heroes

Fiction speaks to children through its characters, but the storytelling medium intervenes in several ways: by selecting which stories to publish or produce, and by presenting its heroes talking out loud or in print, in stationary poses or in action. How available stories are to children varies with the medium too; live theater's characters are hard to come by, while television's excel at being accessible.

Getting an early start

> I know that Big Bird isn't real. That's just a costume. There's just a plain bird inside. (preschool viewer of *Sesame Street*)

Children are 'meeting' television heroes and heroines very early in their lives: there they are, in virtually every home, ready to be seen, heard, and to entertain. When permitted access, two-year-olds will look at television in an active, purposeful way.[18] Toddlers' experience with TV begins with recognizing familiar people, puppets, animals and things. Regularly appearing characters are children's first handles on the flux of programming and commercials. Any deviation from a show's usual cast bewilders two- and three-year-olds and causes them to question even a familiar show's identity.[19] Initially, a character's disappearance from the screen is cause for concern or at least clarification: 'Where Ernie go?' a two-year-old watching *Sesame Street* asks his mother.

Preschool children do figure out early on that relationships with TV characters work only one way: kids can see and hear the people on TV, talk back to them, mimic what they do; but the reverse will not occur. Characters on TV will not reach out through the screen, proffering that nice candy bar or toy. But television personalities still influence young children in many ways and likely will for many years to come.

Modeling more than murder   We fuss and fret about the untoward effects on children's behavior of seeing television heroes so often use physical violence to solve problems. And justifiably. The impetus such televised aggression provides children to commit similar acts is undeniable.[20] Seeing a socially disapproved act like violence rewarded, however briefly, is especially enticing to young viewers. Nonetheless, we must be aware of other behaviors children learn from their favorite TV characters. On-screen activity abounds that might interest a child, and this very eventfulness is what makes television fiction so memorable to them.

TV characters' performances encourage a wide range of behavior among young audiences. Show nursery school children appealing characters who behave affectionately toward others, for example on *Mister Rogers' Neighborhood*, and these young viewers will offer more affection to their schoolmates.[21] Provide kindergarteners with a television diet of programs whose main characters help one another, as on *Lassie* and *The Brady Bunch*, and children will act more helpful, at least temporarily.[22] Even the amount of self-control primary grade students display – how well they obey game rules or respect prohibitions – can be influenced by the way TV characters their age and sex are seen handling similar situations.[23]

Not that children indiscriminately repeat actions they have seen characters perform.[24] They will less often imitate a character whose behavior they see punished, for example, like the villain sent to prison for his crime. The situations children find themselves in after watching a TV performance also modify their reactions: having a watchful parent in the room following a fight scene can effectively inhibit brothers and sisters from recreating a few fast punches. Youngsters' ability to copy a given behavior is a factor too: kindergarteners may be better equipped and more eager to rehearse somersaults than conversations.

Whether or not the behavior is put to immediate use, children are still picking up cues for how to behave just from watching video characters. And what kind of conduct children learn from television depends in large measure on who they like to watch.

Not that children don't observe and become informed by people off screen. Television is by no means the sole source of vicarious learning. Children grow up emulating behavior of parents, teachers and other significant individuals with whom they identify. As one vivid little example, what parent hasn't had his or her every gesture duplicated by a youngster disciplining dolls or pets?

What makes television heroes and heroines newsworthy models for children is that they are a limited sample of perfect strangers.

By highlighting one behavior and downgrading another, preferred TV characters affect the value child fans assign to an action. Take the case of older youngsters who are becoming more socially aware. Television drama offers these audience members previews of social situations they have yet to encounter firsthand. Children approaching adolescence will sometimes acknowledge learning social rules of thumb, such as how to dress or ask for a date, from watching situation comedies and family dramas. As one eleven-year-old put it: 'The things that happen in the show [*Family Affair*] could happen to you, and they show examples of what to say. It's good for parents too, they should watch and see how to treat you.'[25] Even their descriptions of such shows gravitate toward observations about characters' personalities and relationships with others.[26] Of course, the type of program dictates what can be said of its characters. Still, preadolescents are paying more attention to people's social skills, thoughts and motives. Personality traits valued on frequently watched programs can easily gain status in their eyes.

Any medium's fiction can perform this socializing role, be it on stage, on screen, or in print. But access to adult-oriented material in other media is more circumscribed, by the price of admission, by ratings, by publishers, by limits in children's understanding. When it comes to American television, however, many programs intended for adults are also heard, seen and grasped by older youth.

The chicken or the egg problem Children's choice of fictional heroes and heroines is a little like the chicken or the egg problem: which comes first, children's taste in story characters or the currently heralded selection? Clearly the two interact.

On one hand, children's sense of what qualifies as heroism is being shaped by the fiction society offers. More so than for adults, youngsters' ideas of what constitutes not only legitimate but desirable actions, attitudes and appearances are influenced by the stories they encounter. While this influence of fiction has a long tradition, today the most visible folklore is furnished by the relative newcomer, television. Its numerous stories dramatize scenarios of what the world is and should be like. Find out who are your children's favorite characters and what these people seek to accomplish. Are their values consistent with yours? If not, this is one opportunity to voice an opinion or recommend another show.

At the same time, children do weed out those characters who appeal most to their interests, needs and wishes. Children do vote unselfconsciously for their favorite fantasies: only some books are reread, only some movies revisited, only some TV shows are watched in reruns. Parents and other adults close to children play a crucial role in bringing notable, but less heavily advertised characters to their attention.

A word about movie idols

The most formidable story heroes and heroines in many children's eyes are those who appear in the movies. Compared to the everyday alliances that watching television permits, movie going limits young viewers to more occasional and special visits with its stars. Even the term 'star' is arguably best suited to actors and actresses in films; they seem to enjoy more revered status and occupy higher, more glamorous ground. Though a movie's cast may be more distant, they leave their audience no less aroused. On the contrary; the film medium intensifies viewers' participation in a story more than television, with its large-scale photography, uninterrupted plots and lights-out-while-watching policy. While reviewing a theatrical movie on cable TV or VCR effectively reminds you of its characters and what they go through, it does not replicate the more awe-inspiring experience of seeing them perform on the Silver Screen. The difference is one of degree. As a result, children may admire certain TV protagonists, but idolize movie actresses, actors, and the characters they portray.

The genius of TV and movie tie-ins

Children redesign their heroes and heroines in play. Re-enacting even a familiar story, they will add, omit and modify character actions so that the drama elaborated has more personal meaning than the original text or script. The way a story presents its hero identifies him as a character and accounts for his initial appeal. But beyond a certain point, it is a child's own preoccupations and imaginative impulses that inspire the moves made in play.

In these creative endeavors, children are aided and abetted by the toys, dolls and play figures that tie in with release of youth-oriented television programs and movies, from collectible Smurf charms to the entire cast and trappings of the *Star Wars* trilogy. I hate to acknowledge these spinoff items, which offend me for the way they exploit children's enjoyment of a story in the interest of product sales. Yet some of these replica products do serve children's play needs well. Specific character dolls, play figures and detailed props have an appealing authenticity, and this 'realism' suggests settings and schemes children have witnessed on screen but want to explore for themselves. Of course, simpler, more generic toys can be used in their place and may be better designed and more durable. What's important, however, is that children have opportunities to reinvent in play a character who otherwise might overwhelm them. Then the character becomes a tool for dramatizing a child's fantasies, not just the writer's or producer's.

Why do children want to read the novelizations of movies they have already seen? Movie and TV-related books are more and more visible in stores, and they sell. I don't just mean novels with a prior publishing history that later are adapted for film. Frequently the order is now reversed; stories whose first incarnation was film are rewritten and illustrated for the page. Such books' popularity attests to the way one medium presentation can supplement another.[27] Reviewing a film story in print differs qualitatively from revisiting it at the theater. A movie children have enjoyed can be savored and lingered over in a book. In its company, children can summon up not just the scenes and characters, but a milder, more manageable version of the feelings and excitement they evoked. One reason photographs of film frames work so well in these print spinoffs is because they conjure up more vivid associations with the movie than do words. For better or for worse, such highly illustrated books also offer poor readers access to screen stories. The greater control children exercise dealing with a book – the self-paced delivery and more tempered impact of words and still pictures – allows them the time and emotional leeway to re-experience a story on their own terms.

Can parents still be their children's heroines and heroes?

There appear to be more candidate heroines and heroes these days competing for children's attention. Children's ideas in this country are fed by many voices: dress like this, covet my cereal, love me and my music video. Fantasies perpetrated by the media are so well-crafted and wish-fulfilling, it may seem nearly impossible for parents or teachers to reach children with their own messages . . . at least not without the resources of an advertising agency.

Take heart, if you feel that way. There remains no one like a parent (or second, a teacher) to mediate between children and the stories society tells them about itself. No caring adult can abdicate the responsibility, challenging though it may be. Be encouraged by the report that children's interpretation of given television content, for instance, is highly susceptible to communication from parents. Don't hesitate to step in and speak up; not so much to protect your child's affection for you against interlopers – there really is no serious contest – but to offer your own attitudes and values. You may already be doing just that. In-home observations of toddlers reveal that talk about television sometimes begins very early. Here is one mother making a point about humane behavior to her eighteen-month-old:[29]

> Context: *Child is watching a boxing match on TV.*
> Mother: 'Fighting is not nice.
>   Kissing and hugging are nice.'
> Child: 'Not nice, not nice.'

Children do not adopt wholesale the traits of any one model. Fictional heroes and heroines are most likely to hold sway about subjects boys and girls have little experience with firsthand. Be there for children when there is something you want them to know. Provide the information. Whenever possible, model the behaviour that you expect from them, and you will become the hero or heroine they deep down want you to be.

Hands on

Fantasy and reality go hand in hand. Children only laugh at nonsense when they can recognize what is sensible. Fantastic plots are enjoyed partly because they ignore the consensus about what really is possible. The story hero or heroine children wish to be like highlights some trait or behavior they aspire to in real life. Via the characters children know and love, you can help them appreciate both the fanciful and the factual. In the process you will learn more about what children understand of life and the possibilities it holds for them.

Checking children's fantasy savvy

Here are several suggestions for questions to ask and information to offer children about the reality status of the fiction they encounter. Tailor more specific questions and comments to the particular story content and medium.

(1) Is that true? How do you know?

(2) Could that really happen? How can you tell?
Younger children will enjoy pointing out blatant violations of physical reality. As they get older, ask children to make more subtle judgments, such as about the accuracy of biographies, autobiographies, or historical dramas. Ask older youngsters about biases that might exist in news reporting.

(3) Ask older children: Is that likely to happen?

(4) Are people really like that?
Use this question to uncover stereotypes children may have about age, race, sex, nationality, various occupations, etc. Correct their misconceptions. Whenever possible, remind them of someone they know as a counter example.

(5) Ask children about people in TV commercials:
Why is that girl/boy smiling?
Use this question to talk about how, in commercials, advertisers try and persuade you to want their products. Get children in the habit of looking for the ways a commercial shows off its product.

(6) Where do stories come from?
- Help younger children understand how stories in each medium are fabricated. Explain that books are written by people and printed by publishing companies. TV stories and movies are performed by actors and actresses, who play the parts of different characters. Cameras are used to record the stories on videotape or film.
- See if children know the meaning of words like: acting, actor, actress, rehearse, script, sound effect, special visual effect, director.
- Look up unfamiliar words.
- To help explain television production to young children, use *The Bionic Bunny Show*, a picture book by Marc Brown and me (Atlantic Monthly Press, 1984). For a book of eight lessons on television content, try Dorothy Singer *et al.*, *Getting the Most Out of TV* (Goodyear, 1981).

Making up characters

Creating characters with children exercises everyone's imagination. It can also be a lot of fun. Draw on your personal experience and the people, animals, plants, machines, etc., you have known. Tell children to do the same. Be playful.

(1) Creating characters

- Ask children to pick as a character some person, plant, animal, toy or other object. You can limit their choice (fuzzy, four-legged creature; talking robot) or leave it wide open.

- Have children describe their character fully, in writing or orally. What are all the things they know about him/her/it? These might include: what it looks like, how it moves (have them demonstrate), how it talks (have them demonstrate), what it eats, wears, dreams about, likes to do most, never does. What does it want most of all? Encourage details.

- Find out from children where their character lives. Does it have a home? What is its home like? Is this a familiar setting, perhaps their neighborhood, or is it a faraway, even imaginary place?

- Ask children to make their character the heroine or hero of a story. In the story, their character should try and accomplish something worthy of respect – what it is is up to them. Children might suggest a moral for the story, especially if their character changes or learns something new.

(2) Character captioning

- Show children pictures of people or animals with expressive faces or in provocative poses. Use newspaper or magazine photographs, for example.

- Have children choose a picture to elaborate a character for. You can follow the instructions in (1).

- Compare different descriptions given for the same picture.

(3) Comparing character incarnations

- Find a story in the library which has been illustrated more than once, such as *The Sleeping Beauty, Beauty and the Beast*, collections of fairy tales, *Aesop Fables, The Velveteen Rabbit*.

- First read the story aloud without using pictures.

- Then show children alternative ways characters have been pictured. Ask them which rendering they like best to go with the story. Have them explain why they made the choice they did.

(4) Disguises and transformations

- Ask children: If you could be anyone or anything, who or what would

115

you be? You can limit the choice (animal, person, object) or leave it wide open.

- Have them tape record or write a story or even draw a picture about what they would do if they were. . . .

- Don't wait for Hallowe'en. Children enjoy devising disguises any time of year. Help them with costumes and masks by making available old clothes, makeup, hats, sheets, towels, boxes and bags before discarding. Give them access to scissors, markers, tape and string.

- Show children how to make paper dolls. The figure should be drawn and cut from cardboard or other sturdy material. Measure clothes against figure before you cut. Leave extra tabs to attach clothing to figure.

Rating heroes and heroines

Keep up-to-date with your children's heroes and heroines. They are sources not only of information but inspiration, not only of vicarious adventure, but also of values.

(1) Polling children's favorites
- Take a vote among children. Who is your favorite:

TV character	singer or music group
movie character	author
book character	artist
actor	scientist or inventor
actress	political leader
athlete	person in neighborhood

Poll as many or few categories as seems appropriate. For fun, you might also have them nominate several 'worst' candidates.

- Elicit reasons for their choices.

- If polling takes place in school, let children tally the votes and post results. Consider it like the school (grade or class) 'Top 40' or Nielsen ratings. Have a fall and spring vote.

(2) Young critics
- Discuss with older children what they think makes a character interesting. For example, a totally predictable character can be boring.

- Interrupt a story children are listening to. Take a vote on what the protagonist will do next. How much agreement is there among chldren? How many guess correctly?

116

- Have children critique each other's stories the same way, if possible.
- Have children try and add humor to a serious story or make a simple character mysterious.
- Can they turn an evil character into a virtuous one? Do they have to change both actions and motives?

Chapter 8

When computers get into the storytelling act

Do you worry that your children will be functionally illiterate because they don't know how to program a computer? On the other hand, perhaps you fear that, once so skilled, they will want to hear their bedtime story from a machine instead of you. Or take video war games too seriously. Coping with the new electronic media may put you square between the devil and the deep blue sea.

Don't let a little confusion alarm you. Exposure to new media invariably entails feeling your way, taking risks in order to discover opportunities. Getting perspective on any technology's usefulness to children is challenging. And a new technology's products are often primitive, their outcomes untested. This is uncharted territory. Listen to a software salesperson wax ecstatic over this season's product line and to a skeptical teacher who has seen too much expensive audiovisual equipment relegated to the closet. See if you don't hear different futures predicted for the so-called computer revolution in education. Those of you pioneer parents and educators who investigate these technologies for yourselves will not only benefit from firsthand knowledge; by making choices and voicing opinions, you also will help determine how fully these emerging media realize their potential to help children learn.

This chapter focuses on various partnerships among computers, video and print. When do they contribute something unique to the art of storytelling or duplicate the performance of other media? Will using computers change how children process, learn from and enjoy a story? Since some of this discussion is still only speculative – the verdict simply isn't in – it is more important to help you raise good questions than to answer them too glibly.

Who is telling whom a story?

One of the most striking ways electronic media distinguish themselves as storytellers is by blurring the boundary between teller and audience. In the past the two roles have been separate: audio recordings speak, children listen; television broadcasts, children watch (and listen). Even when a child interrupts a live narration and finishes telling the tale himself, one person is still the teller, the other the tellee. With computers getting into the storytelling act, this is no longer necessarily so.

The following array of electronic media vary in the extent to which children participate in the delivery of a story, and in the words, pictures, or other symbols they use. What children take away from these new forms of fiction is likely to vary as well.

Video cassette recorder   Because the video cassette recorder (VCR) can be used to tape television shows off the air, to view prerecorded cassettes, and, with the addition of a camera, to tape new material, it liberates audiences from the broadcast schedule.[1]

Children who help decide what to record and when to watch are exercising control over their exposure to television fiction. They can be more selective about viewing, picking a story to watch more like they would a book to read. A program on tape can be seen at home when chores are done or at school when it fits into the lesson instead of only during prime time. A taped story can also be reviewed in much the same way a novel is reread. Many VCRs are equipped with fast and slow motion in forward and reverse, stop-action, and single-frame advance, features that give young viewers' access to video stories a flexibility akin to page turning. Children can slow down a scene to savor it, skip images they don't like, check a story's ending before they begin.

Should we expect differences in what content children learn from

VCR-viewed stories as opposed to those seen on broadcast or cable TV? Probably not, because it's only the logistics of viewing that have changed, not the story itself. (Prerecorded cassettes do expand the selection of fiction available to home and schools.) The places to look for and encourage changes from VCR use are in children's viewing habits and attitude toward video. Furthermore, if children bring more selectivity and purpose to their small screen viewing, they may, in turn, attend more closely to video stories and get more out of them.

Computer software A computer's software consists of the various programs or sets of directions it uses to carry out different tasks.[2] All programs, whether cassettes, disks, or cartridges, are recordings of electronic information.

Computer-assisted instruction The computer software most widely used in today's classrooms is of the type that delivers information, questions students about it, and then checks their answers. Much like an electronic workbook, the content of such computer-aided instruction (CAI) is specified and directed by the program. Student input is solicited, but usually restricted to indicating answers from the choices offered. If a child gives a wrong response, the computer may provide a hint or explanation. Correct answers are sometimes rewarded with access to games or other appealing activities. More 'intelligent' programs take account of a student's choices when branching to the next portion of instruction.

By interrupting text appearing on screen, CAI programs can quiz children for different kinds of prose learning. In the simple example below, users are asked to infer a word's meaning from referent words in the previous sentence.[3]

Using computers this way to tutor children about fiction serves certain educational goals. For example, training children in vocabulary, inference making, and recall of important events fosters their story comprehension. Such CAI programs are a convenient resource for teachers because they can help teach the existing curriculum. Properly equipped computers can present story content using not only printed text but vocal speech, pictures, animation, even sound effects, thus testing children's skills in reading, listening and viewing. While answering questions posed about prose is a common classroom activity, the interaction between tutor and pupil in a computer lesson is unique. On one hand, the computer is as patient and objective as a workbook. Each child can proceed at his or her own pace and level of competence. At the same time, the computer's flexibility and responsiveness makes working on one more like communicating with another intelligent agent; and until now, that agent has

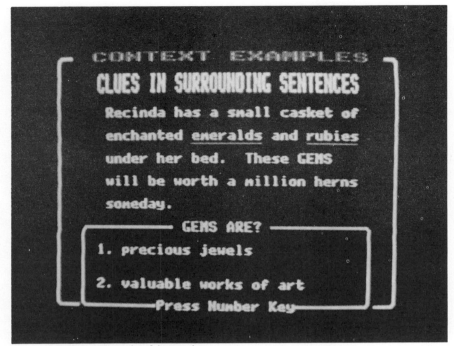

Figure 8.1 Computer-assisted instruction

always been a person! Learning on a computer is more motivating for some students and therefore more effective.

But computerizing this traditional teaching function takes little advantage of a computer's potential.[4] The computer is primarily a vehicle for delivering a story in words, pictures and sounds rather than a storytelling medium with its own distinct features. The CAI program simply incorporates a lesson into the story it tells. The only way such a computer lesson in fiction distinguishes itself as a learning experience is by giving children practice in running a simple program.

Adventure games: simulating fictional worlds The adventures children play on computers marry fiction to a game format. In varying degrees these games redefine story as a collaboration between computer program and player.

(1) *Video games* Your combatant is a spacecraft, your mission to blow up alien vehicles before they destroy you. As you progress through the game's levels or screens, aliens appear more often and move less

121

predictably, making your job more difficult. Like a conventional board game, this typical video game scenario challenges its players to accomplish some goal, leaving obstacles and opportunities in their path. The game player takes charge of one or more pieces or 'actors' whose activities must conform to certain rules. In Monopoly each person is responsible for one actor's enterprise. A chess player monitors movements for sixteen pieces who vary in rank from king to pawn. In video or arcade-style games, players usually confront many more figures and scenes. The content of video games takes a graphic form. Computers using high resolution graphics or video disk images can present detailed and fully animated figures. Adventures take place on the screen in two- or three-dimensional space. In 2-D, figures move up and down, right and left; those in 3-D can also move forward and back.

These game figures are known mostly by the actions they can perform and the conditions under which they can act, rather than by their personality or morality.[5] It is premature to call them dramatic characters or their predicaments stories, however, as engaging as putting them through their paces may be. Rather, the actors in most video game adventures face a series of circumstances, often perilous ones, to which they respond with unambiguous, physical means. These adventures are fast-paced contests in which the timing of a player's reactions is critical and dexterity more important than strategy. Stop to weigh alternatives or consider your actor's motives, and you're dead meat.

What do children learn from playing video adventures? First let's tease apart game content from form. Important as a video game's particular mission is in setting the tone of an adventure – parents are justified in rejecting a game whose goals are offensive[6] – it is certainly not inherent to the medium. Video adventures could require cooperative actions to achieve some goal rather than combative ones. For example, players might coordinate events on screen to help actors survive a tornado or to rescue someone trapped in a fire. It is much more fundamental that the outcome of a player's actions be quickly visible and sustain children's interest.

Playing most video games entails keeping track of rapidly changing visual displays. To manipulate an object effectively requires recognizing where it is in space and from what point of view it is shown. Now add movement: game players need to know not only where a figure is right now, but how fast and in what direction it is traveling. Multiply all this by the number of figures players must monitor.

Because of the perceptual activities involved, video game playing likely helps children develop spatial skills and eye-hand coordination. Research with children is scant, but young adults' scores on video games have been found related to those on standardized spatial skills tests.[7] For example, players' performance on a three-dimensional video game correlated with their ability to visualize an object's rotation in three-dimensional space. But this evidence doesn't tell us which came first, spatial skills or game playing. More promising is the finding that practice with video games can improve a player's spatial aptitude scores.[8] The fast-paced reactions called for in these games may force young and old players alike to think visually rather than in verbal, analytic terms. Video games are in fact being used in diverse settings to train and measure spatial skills; for example, the US Army has adopted upgraded versions of video games to train soldiers in gunnery and tank maneuvers on the battlefield. Spatial skills are also important in math, science, engineering and the visual arts.[9]

Video game playing calls on children to think inductively. Unlike conventional games, where the rules are made available before players begin, in most video games children go right to the screen, discovering the rules and regularities of the game as they play. By observing the outcomes of their different attempts, children learn to navigate a game figure through various obstacles. (Hints for playing are also passed on by word of mouth.) Therein lies part of the challenge and excitement of the game; each video adventure is something of a mystery that players must unravel in order to succeed.

Letting children play electronic adventure games is one way to introduce them to computers. It's easier to acquire a skill when you get pleasure from practicing it over and over. Many children enjoy playing video games and gain experience using computers in the process. But remember that with this kind of software, the game – not the child – still calls the shots, and what children think they can do with computers will be limited to a narrow range of activities.

(2) *Interactive fiction*

> Shipwrecked! Fritz, you and your family are perched precariously atop rocks just off the coast of a remote tropical island. How will you get everyone safely ashore? Once on land, will you have the skill and ingenuity to survive in the wilderness? Can you cleverly devise a way to be rescued?

So introduced, this software challenges prospective players to solve the problems caused by a family's accident at sea.[10] If the adventure's premise sounds familiar, it should; this computer game is an adaptation of the classic novel, *The Swiss Family Robinson*. The young boy and most of his family are there, the tropical island setting is there with its wild animals and exotic plants, even the dominant theme – survival in the wilderness – is retained. What differs is children's involvement in the plot.

Interactive computer fiction demands that children participate. Instead of reacting to a preselected sequence of fictional events, now a fund of narrative information waits to be ordered. Choosing the hero's next steps becomes a job shared between player and program designer. By commanding their character to perform certain actions and seeing what each decision brings, children try and forge a safe, successful path through an adventure. They accumulate information in the process about characters, settings and events, piecing together a story terrain much as they would a puzzle. Whether searching for treasure, crossing the old American west, or surviving on a deserted island, exploring this kind of responsive simulated world involves detective work. One constructs a version of a tale, rather than witnessing it take a single predetermined shape.

One important reason to distinguish between interactive fiction and the video adventures just described, both of which belong in the same game family, is because of the different activities each of them entails. Notice how in the example above, the game begins with a still screen of printed text, rather than an array of moving objects already in pursuit of some target. The time constraints imposed on video game players – act now, think later – are absent in interactive fiction. Now a child can take as much time as he or she needs to read the screen for information.

Children's encounters with interactive computer fiction are like problem solving exercises. Young players must consider alternative courses of action, choose needed props, and use clues that will help them reach each goal. In the screen below, for example, players can discover various ways to avoid the danger of an approaching python (curved shape on the right).[11]

This variety of game software is called educational because succeeding in these adventures requires that children learn something deemed academically useful. In the process of seeking information, for instance, children may recognize what are good questions to ask. When answers are given in printed text, they are also practicing reading comprehension.

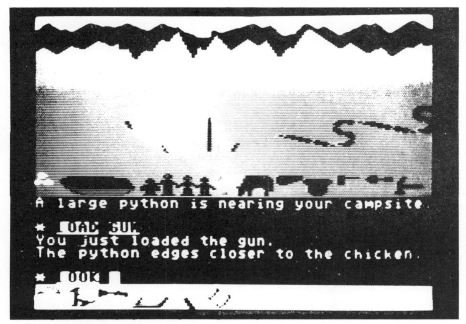

A large python is nearing your campsite.

* LOAD GUN
You just loaded the gun.
The python edges closer to the chicken.

* LOOK

Figure 8.2 Interactive computer fiction

In the course of remembering pertinent details, children can learn about a wide range of subjects. Moreover, they could be dealing not only with words, but pictures, maps, mazes, or numbers. Unfortunately, what is or isn't learned from these games has yet to be documented. Nor is all available interactive fiction software so progressive. With many if not most programs, players still move through an adventure in linear fashion, making decisions the same way they would on a multiple choice test. But the potential is there to design games that let children manipulate story content on the computer using all kinds of symbols and procedures.

Playing with hypothetical events this way may sharpen children's understanding of what it takes to make a story. Interactive fiction players are constantly encountering new situations and having to make decisions 'in character.' To make well-informed decisions requires taking into account specific fictional conditions, whether these pertain to realistic or fantastic settings, whether cast in past, present, or future times. Children also may identify more with a fictional hero or heroine over whose fate they exercise some control.

Then again, being able to affect an adventure's outcome may break down its integrity as a story in children's eyes and undo that quality of

125

inevitability an audience waits for and enjoys. Perhaps some of the magic that has for so long accompanied storytelling will dissipate once children participate in this process, once there is no single way to proceed. Still, computer game playing evokes its own sense of drama. Like meeting someone for the first time, there is a fascination in contending with a new program without knowing what kind of dialogue to expect.

In the end we may find children's story appreciation not affected at all. To them, very likely computer games are one thing, stories quite another. The two may never be compared. Whatever influence on children's sense of story computer adventures turn out to have, their use is clearly moving children into the fiction-making enterprise.

General purpose tools Ultimately roles shift so that children are the storytellers and computers the facilitators, there to help edit, illustrate, evan animate stories youngsters invent. Most tool software enables users to enter, organize and revise information of a certain kind: words in the case of word processors, musical notes and rhythms with music editing systems, pictures and designs with graphic editors. Like brushes, paint and canvas, general purpose tools define an activity broadly without specifying its content. For computer users, however, the emphasis is on wielding symbols, not physical materials.

(1) *Word processors* Word processing programs are tools for writing and editing text. Once children type in their draft, it appears on the screen for review. Commands made using the keyboard move a cursor (blinking light on screen) forward, back, up and down, letting young writers point to words they want to change. Further commands allow writers to add, insert, erase and move text around.[12] In this way children can easily correct spelling, grammar, punctuation, and content without having to retype the whole piece. Children equipped with a printer can transfer their writing to paper. The computer will follow instructions for making a clean, well-formatted copy, setting margins, spacing lines, underlining and the like.

Word processors fit into the existing school curriculum more readily than many games and other software.[13] Although generally more expensive, they also are more versatile. Word processors assist children individually with their written work and expedite more social uses of writing. Composing with keyboard and screen seems to make collaboration among students physically easier; a pair of young writers can sit together at the computer, sharing the tasks of typing, correcting and generating ideas.[14] Properly equipped systems can also be used to exchange electronic mail; putting distant classrooms in touch with each

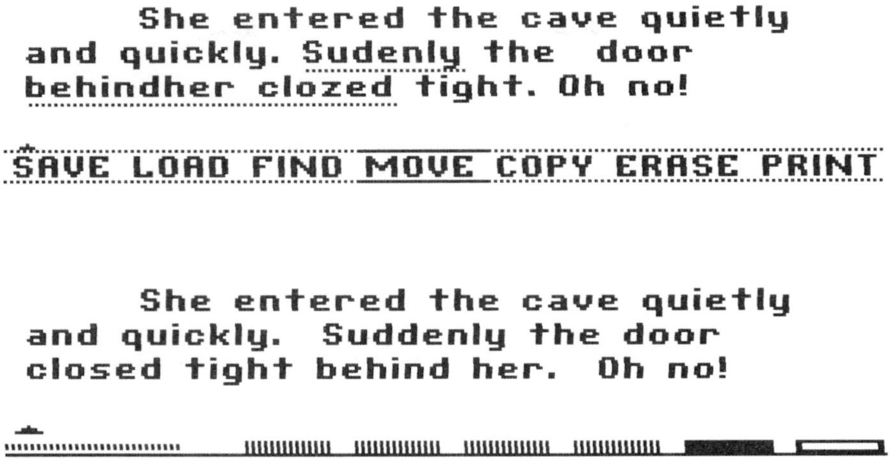

```
      She entered the cave quietly
 and quickly. Sudenly the  door
 behindher clozed tight. Oh no!
```

```
SAUE LOAD FIND MOVE COPY ERASE PRINT
```

```
      She entered the cave quietly
 and quickly.  Suddenly the door
 closed tight behind her.  Oh no!
```

Figure 8.3 Word processor

other via computer can motivate students to write, and rewrite, with an audience in mind.[15]

But do children write better stories or different kinds of stories using a word processor? It really is too soon to say. Early research evaluating children's use of word processors leaves me cautious yet optimistic. When adequately prepared, children seem to do more revising on a word processor. For example, one group of sixth graders with previous editing experience corrected more errors in spelling, punctuation and syntax revising their stories using a word processor than they did using pencil and paper.[16] And eighth grade students working on word processors over several weeks not only made similar corrections in spelling and grammar, but changed paragraph structure – something they rarely would otherwise do. They also spent more time composing their text than was customary with paper and pen.[17]

On one hand, any help we can give children in editing their writing is cause for celebration, they do so little of it. Elementary school students' typical strategy is to try and make a composition correct the first time. They don't like to recopy by hand. If children prepare a second draft on paper, it is with an eye toward producing a neater, more legible copy than the first, not a better written one. It is no easy job to find the words to express your thoughts and, at the same time, negotiate rules of spelling, grammar and punctuation.

On the other hand, these young writers are using word processors primarily for correcting minor mistakes, not for improving content. They tend to appreciate word processors for such simple virtues as: 'when you erase, you don't rip the paper.' In general, students compose the same way with a word processor as without one.[18] They begin writing the first sentence and proceed straight through to the last, doing little rearranging in between. They still don't consider making the kinds of structural and substantive changes a word processor facilitates.

We must remember, however, this is a new technology for children. For children's writing to be affected by it, they will first need to become comfortable and fairly competent using both computer and word processing programs, which takes time. The fact that students in these short-term studies produced shorter compositions on computer than on paper suggests they have not yet achieved that level of skill.[19]

But even when children have mastered its use, a word processor cannot teach them to write better stories. It only provides a more efficient way to make changes in text. So far, improvements in the quality and effectiveness of children's writing on a word processor have resulted only when they also had a teacher's or computer-based editorial support.[20] In other words, for young writers' work to benefit from using the word processor, they must approach the computer informed about writing and revising a story or receive outside help while they compose.

(2) *Graphics tools*   Some computer systems offer children tools to create graphics on screen. Prominent among these are paint systems which allow users to draw lines, paint in areas with pattern or color, duplicate, magnify and relocate images. These tools can be operated several different ways. A young artist can draw with a stylus attached to a separate graphics tablet and have the image transfer to the screen. Alternatively he or she can roll a small device called a 'mouse' along a table-top to direct the cursor's path on the screen. Children also can generate pictures and designs using certain programming languages like LOGO.[21] Here they must learn to type in precise commands (Repeat 4 (Forward 75 Right 90)) and watch their product (a square in this case) materialize on screen. LOGO procedures are used to direct the movements of either a 'light turtle' marker on the screen or a mechanical 'floor turtle.' Note: you move a mouse to direct the computer, whereas your commands to the computer direct a turtle.

It remains to be seen how using a computer to make pictures and other graphics will affect children's art. Perhaps some children will always feel more at home drawing on paper, while others will come to prefer the precision and procedural economy possible with the computer. Observers have noticed such individual biases budding even at the preschool level, where some children, but not others, are creating more highly detailed and articulated pictures on the computer than on paper.[22] For children attracted to the medium of computer graphics, its resources can serve them well illustrating stories. They can easily experiment, edit, even animate their pictures of characters and scenes, eventually printing out copies to use.

Both graphics tools and word processors are designed to help users accomplish what they want to do; children, parents and teachers set the agenda rather than the program. Furthermore, these experiences model adult uses of computers; using general purpose tools, more than most games and CAI, helps prepare youngsters to deal with the computer's real-world applications.

Defining computer literacy

Dealing with machines as responsive and well-informed as computers raises provocative questions for children. Several children were overheard by psychologist Sherry Turkle speculating as follows about the intelligence and existential status of a computerized toy called Merlin:[23]

> *Craig (age 6):* 'Merlin doesn't know if it cheats. It won't know if it breaks. It doesn't know if you break it, Robert. It's not alive.'
> *Greg (age 8):* 'Someone taught Merlin to play. But he doesn't know if he wins or loses.'
> *Robert (age 7):* 'Yes he does know if he loses. He makes different noises.'
> *Greg:* 'No, stupid. It's smart. It's smart enough to make the right kinds of noises. But it doesn't really know if it loses. That's how you can cheat it. It doesn't know you are cheating. And when it cheats, it doesn't even know it's cheating.'
> *Jenny (age 6):* 'Greg, to cheat you have to know you are cheating.'

What do you want your children to understand about the computer? What kinds of experience and competence with computers is it important for them to have? Taking time to think about these questions can help you sort out in your own mind what being literate with computers should mean.

Let's review the range of computer skills it is possible to attain.[24] Starting at the unskilled, nonuser end are those children and adults who have indirect contact with machines, such as cash registers at supermarkets, without realizing they contain computers. Once you show youngsters how to manage even a microwave oven or automatic bank teller, however, they become 'end-users' who can follow fixed procedures on a computer to accomplish some task. Children who interact with CAI programs or play video games, if they do nothing more, will have end-user experience. Strictly speaking, most of the software discussed in this chapter requires this level of skill, which attests to how broad it can be. Even though a word processor allows for great flexibility in its use, children are still working with a program someone else has designed.

Being a skilled user of computer programs is a little like being a good driver. Get behind the wheel, and your car usually gets you where you want to go; never mind you don't know how it works or even how to fix it. Likewise, the ability to operate various computer programs will probably serve most children's needs well enough. The Bureau of Labor Statistics estimates that, at least in the near future, only a relatively small number of jobs will require higher level computer skills.[25] Moreover, specific job skills can be learned as they are needed.

If children who use computer programs effectively are behind the wheel, then those who write programs are under the hood and eventually at the drawing board, planning next year's models. Knowing how to program a computer occurs at many levels of expertise. It begins with students learning a computer language's common commands (semantics) and rules for their use (syntax), composing a simple program with this vocabulary – to draw a square, Repeat 4 (Forward 75 Right 90) – and finding errors or 'bugs' – Repeat 4 instead of 3 – that prevent it from working. It ends with those programmers who can fix and design software for other people to use.

Without some firsthand experience writing their own programs, it is argued, children will not appreciate the special logic that is a computer. (Try rereading this sentence substituting for 'computer' words like 'book' and 'television.') Like young Robert in the dialogue above, they may overestimate a computer's knowledge or be confused about its source.

Learning to program a computer is also credited with cultivating certain thinking skills.[26] The systematic planning that programming demands – inventing small procedures that gradually build a solution to a larger problem, expressing each step precisely, testing their correctness, recognizing possible alternative solutions – this behavior is said to help children solve problems in other domains. So far, there is meager evidence for these claims. For one thing, this kind of analytic, self-conscious thinking is acquired more readily when children are older. Furthermore, students will need more experience programming, and possibly instruction in using these skills in different situations, before any transfer will occur.

Literacy is the ability to read and write. But what level of performance that implies is open to debate. Where the line is drawn usually reflects the importance a society assigns to the language in question. This is particularly challenging with a medium like the computer, which can speak so many languages and present information using so many kinds of symbols.[27] Certainly, we want children to not just survive the computer's emergence in our culture, but fully exploit and enjoy it. But then, who is going to be responsible for teaching children the languages of yet another medium?

Hands on

Getting started with computers

(1) *Give yourself a frame of reference*   If you are thinking of buying a computer but still feel confused or intimidated, here is one way to get a little footing. Imagine for a minute that you are shopping for something more familiar instead, such as stereo components or a new set of tools. Mentally review the kinds of things you will want to consider:

- What jobs can this system perform?
- How up-to-date is it?
- How powerful?
- How hard or easy is each piece to operate?
- Can its uses be extended in the future?
- Who will service this equipment?
- How much does it cost?

The same basic questions will serve you well looking for a computer.

(2) *Move out into computer territory*   Find out what is available in personal and home computers. There is a lot of hardware to choose from, but it varies in what it can do and how well.

- Memory is a key factor. How much memory does a computer have? Or, more accurately, how much data can it store and manipulate? Can its memory be extended? Memory is measured in units called bytes: a computer with 64K has the capacity to handle 64,000 bytes.

Compare computers for other features, such as:

- How do they produce graphics, and how detailed (what resolution) can their pictures be?
- Can they produce music and speech?
- How does it feel typing on their keyboard?
- How portable are they?
- Exactly what parts are needed to run a certain program?
- How much will it cost altogether?

Be resourceful getting the information you need.

- Bookstores are full of beginner guides to computers, or you can borrow a book from the library.
- Talk to friends, relatives and co-workers who have some experience with home computers. Your children can be a good source of information too.
- Visit computer stores and ask for demonstrations. Computers are sold not only in specialty stores but in many hi fi and department stores. Don't be afraid to ask for explanations. There is a lot of jargon you may need to have defined.
- Try different models yourself. There is no substitute for firsthand experience.

(3) *Consider your children*   Step back from the computer scene and review the options in terms of your children's aptitudes, interests and needs. (Of course, you may already have their needs in mind when you survey the marketplace.) This also will help you decide which software to start out with.

- What symbols (numbers, words, maps, pictures, etc.) do your children need practice with? Which ones do they have special interest in?
- Do you want them to learn a programming language?
- Do you want to expose them to a variety of software?

132

- Is the computer to be used by children for school work, for leisure, or both?
- What kind of computer, if any, do children use at school? Take this into account if a home computer is to assist them with school-related projects and homework.
- Talk with your children about having a computer at home. How much experience using a computer do they have? What are their expectations about using one?
- Do not neglect the girls!
- Will other family members use the computer? How?

(4) *Return for a possible purchase*   When you have some information under your belt about computers and your family's needs for one, return to the store and look again. This may be a good time to have along children and other family members who are prospective users. Remember your budget, but don't be shortsighted about a computer's usefulness in your home.

Living with a computer

Once you get it home and decide where it goes, now what?

(1) *Setting reasonable limits*   Gaining access to a computer at home is like receiving a wonderful new toy or game; in the excitement, it's easy to let everything else go. And using a computer is especially absorbing. Children may need help fitting computer time into their schedule so that other important activities don't suffer. Learn from your children's experience with another highly entertaining medium, television. Try to prepare for the computer's arrival and avoid problems of overuse and use at inappropriate times. Setting reasonable limits is even more necessary if more than one person will be using the computer at home.

(2) *Learning along with a child*   You and your youngsters may both be beginners when the computer comes into the house, particularly if your children are young. (Older kids may in fact be teaching you.) Your mutual ignorance presents an unusual opportunity: share moments of frustration, share the satisfaction of figuring out what to do next, collaborate and compare learning styles. In a word, participate. This is a time not to be embarrassed to admit 'I don't know.' Try and have access to someone with more experience; but don't be surprised if your helpful expert is under age twenty-one.

Chapter 9

Conclusion

To help any child successfully navigate childhood takes a great deal of confidence. Yet many adults feel unsure of their ability these days: parents seek out experts to help them counsel their own children, teachers struggle to keep their curricula relevant to students' experience, librarians stretch to provide an ever-expanding array of resources. While it is healthy for individuals and institutions to review current practices with an eye toward where improvements can be made, too much doubt weakens anyone's performance.

In terms of sheer quantity, there is more information available to keep up with now, and it is easy to feel overwhelmed. The media are partly responsible. New technologies combining computers, video and print make it possible to communicate faster and faster. Telephone and satellite systems exchange messages between increasingly distant audiences. Who can hope to be up-to-date when many new publications and products are out-of-date before they leave the store? Nor do adults necessarily command respect for being the experts: now that children have access to more media, we may find ourselves learning from someone not even half our age how to operate a computer, assemble a robot, or predict which movies will have the highest box office sales.

The pace of everyday life also has quickened, leaving many of us distracted and out of breath. We use time-saving appliances to get through household chores, take less time to travel from place to place, feel more temporary about professions, possessions and even partners. Many adults are bringing up children alone. These are changing times with fewer rules and standards to fall back on.

But some things in life never change.

Any adult who cares about children points out to them those things he or she values and thinks are important to know. The inclination to teach – and with it the confidence to try and bring out the best in a child – are always there, waiting to be developed. Parents inherit the assignment, while for teachers and other professionals it is a chosen occupation.

Having read this book, you can better appreciate the many ways that literature and media affect your children's development. You should now feel comfortable to approach *any* medium, knowing you have solid grounds on which to evaluate its usefulness. To help in that process, I have offered answers to three basic questions: What is distinctive about a medium's storytelling? What are children of different ages likely to learn, enjoy, and misunderstand about fiction in a given medium? and how can children's story experiences in a medium be enriched?

You don't have to keep track of every juvenile movie, magazine and music video to help youngsters make the most of their various encounters with fiction. However, I have proposed three roles for you to adopt when dealing with young people's experiences with the media. While these are 'hats' I recommend you don, they are also presented as a way to step back and think about how each storytelling medium might best contribute to your children's lives.

(1) Historian Beware of simplistic debates about which medium is *best* and cultivate a sense of perspective. As I have reviewed in some detail, all storytelling media are characterized by both merits and drawbacks. Their value in a given situation depends a lot on how they are used and for whom. Keep in mind that media come and go, or, more often, fade in and out of the limelight: video cassettes are on the upswing, silent films are in the closest. Every generation identifies with the latest tools, technologies and tales. Many American children today feel possessive about computer technology. Which medium will excite children twenty years from now is a matter of conjecture. The stories produced in each

medium have an even more transient existence: some do endure and become classics, but many more are relegated to the back shelves and are soon forgotten.

Learn from the past, but don't live in it. Be open to new media and their fiction. Instead of feeling defensive, retain a healthy skepticism. Reserve judgment until a new product proves itself useful or pleasing in some distinct way. New doesn't always mean better, it only holds that promise. Don't be embarrassed if you need more information about media equipment or other materials. Read reviews, ask other people, and try things out for yourself.

Trust your judgment; it is the product of years of experience. Share your ideas with children. Say why you think a movie is disappointing or a new TV program an improvement. Don't be shaken from your conviction because your favorite novels aren't on the bestseller list. Be original. That adults have standards for fiction is important for youngsters to know; never mind whether they agree with your every opinion. Exercising a sense of history will not only guide your own decisionmaking, but also show children an attitude toward media which they can benefit from all their lives.

(2) Chef Who knows which hero or heroine will capture a child's imagination? Ensure that your children become captivated by many protagonists by giving them a wide assortment of stories to chose from. Expose them to fiction as you would to food, neither all vegetables nor all desserts. Sample many genres, starting when children are young: let them taste of fairy tales and realistic stories, science fiction and historical fiction, mysteries, funny stories, stories with unhappy endings. Allow children to see themselves reflected in all kinds of characters: old and new, rebellious and well-behaved, courageous and cowardly, brawny and brainy.

Prepare the well-balanced media meal: encourage children to watch video and movies, listen to records and tapes, read books, magazines and comics, play computer games. Take them to see live theater, so they can experience the immediacy of an actor's performance.

Teach children to express their own opinions about stories. As they get older, they will have more experience to draw upon when criticizing fiction. Compare different story-lines. Reconcile conflicting versions of the same plot. If children are articulate enough to argue about which fast-food restaurant chain makes the best burger, why not also which movie was better and why? Help them to appreciate how both form and content contribute to a story's effectiveness. This is challenging, since we all seek out meaning and try not to let form get in our way. But many older children are curious about how people in the media do their work and welcome information about production style and technique.

Feeding children a varied diet of fiction serves another purpose by preventing their concept of a story from becoming too limited. It helps them develop a broad appetite for stories – or at least keeps them willing to try something new on the menu.

(3) Traffic cop Variety is not possible without moderation. Children need adults' help to balance not just their diets but their schedules: 'You can watch television, but only after you finish your homework;' 'You can stay up reading, but not all night.' Imposing a rigid daily regime is not the point; rather it is to have a child's life not revolve for too long around a single media activity, be it villainous televison or even the virtuous book. Protecting children from a current burning passion is likely to meet with resistance. Sustaining this kind of structure admittedly takes effort.

But there is more at stake than children's ability to appreciate a good story. Basic mental skills are either encouraged or neglected, depending on the medium. As I said earlier, exposure to any medium's stories requires that children practice interpreting language, pictures, music, or other symbols. Fiction also offers children insight into social relationships and the human psyche. This learning goes on wherever children encounter stories, both in and out of school. It is no accident that most teaching methods are multimedia; the teacher who speaks, gestures, writes on the chalkboard and shows illustrations to explain a new concept acknowledges students' various aptitudes.

There are several occasions, however, when focusing children's attention on one medium is useful. For example, extra practice using a medium can upgrade a low level of skill; compulsive video game players can improve their ability to visualize moving objects in space. Reliance on one medium also can compensate for weakness in using another; children with poor reading skills depend more on illustrations to make sense of stories in print. Finally, extra practice using a medium can foster budding talent; children who produce capable drawings profit from time spent with pictures and graphics. Specialization becomes particularly appropriate as youngsters get older and more serious about their interests.

Children's time with media needs to be balanced by firsthand experience: 'That's enough on the computer for today, now go out and play.' Only then do children get the chance to personalize other people's fantasies. Only by experiencing life firsthand do they have a basis for judging a story's credibility.

CONCLUSION

We want children to be more than a good audience. We share stories with the young so that they will also grow up to be productive, imaginative, caring people – people who know how to take full advantage of all the media, without having to deride their parents' old pleasures or fear their own children's new toys.

Notes

Chapter 1: Why the medium matters

1 Marshall McLuhan, *Understanding Media: The Extensions of Man* (New York: McGraw-Hill, 1964), p. 57.

2 Susan B. Neuman and Peter Prowda, 'Television viewing and reading achievement,' *Journal of Reading* (April 1982), pp. 666-70.

3 See discussion by David R. Olson and Jerome S. Bruner, 'Learning through experience and learning through media,' in D. R. Olson, ed., *Media and Symbols: The Forms of Expression, Communication, and Education* (Chicago: National Society for the Study of Education, 1974), p. 149.

4 Gavriel Salomon, 'Internalization of filmic schematic operations in interaction with learners' aptitudes,' *Journal of Educational Psychology* (66, 4, 1974), pp. 499-511. See also Gavriel Salomon, *Interaction of Media, Cognition, and Learning* (San Francisco: Jossey-Bass, 1979).

5 Wilbur Schramm, ed., *Quality in Instructional Television* (Honolulu: University Press of Hawaii, 1972).

6 See, for example, Thomas Carothers and Howard Gardner, 'When children's drawings become art: the emergence of aesthetic production and perception,' *Development Psychology* (15, 5, 1979), pp. 570-80; and Howard Gardner, 'Children's sensitivity to painting styles,' *Child Development* (41, 1970), pp. 813-21.

7 Arthur N. Applebee, *The Child's Concept of Story: Ages Two to Seventeen* (Chicago: University of Chicago Press, 1978), chapter 3.

8 This charcterization of young children's thinking draws on Jerome S. Bruner, *Beyond the Information Given: Studies in the Psychology of Knowing* (New York: W. W. Norton, 1973), chapter 19; and Jean Piaget, *The Psychology of Intelligence*, trans. by M. Piercy and D. E. Berlyne, 2nd edn (Totowa, New Jersey: Littlefield, Adams, 1973), chapters 3 and 5.

9   Hope Kelly, 'Reasoning about realities: children's evaluations of television and books,' in H. Kelly and H. Gardner, eds, *New Directions for Child Development: Viewing Children Through Television* no. 13 (San Francisco: Jossey-Bass, 1981).

10   See W. Howard Levie and Richard Lentz, 'Effects of text illustrations: a review of research,' *Educational Communication and Technology Journal* (*30*, 1982), pp.195-232; and Joel R. Levin and Alan M. Lesgold, 'On pictures in prose,' *Educational Communication and Technology Journal* (*26*, 3, 1978), pp. 233-43.

11   Kathy Pezdek and Ellen Stevens, 'Children's memory for auditory and visual information on television,' *Developmental Psychology* (*20*, 1984), pp. 212-18.

12   Kelly, 'Reasoning about realities,' p. 68.

13   See, for example, W. Andrew Collins, 'Children's comprehension of television content,' in E. Wartella, ed., *Children Communicating: Media and Development of Thought, Speech, Understanding* (Beverly Hills: Sage, 1979); and Constance Schmidt and Scott Paris, 'Children's use of successive clues to generate and monitor inferences,' *Child Development* (*54*, 1983), pp. 742-59.

14   See, for example, Dorothy Flapan, *Children's Understanding of Social Interaction* (New York: Teachers College Press, 1968).

15   Shelley Rubin and Howard Gardner, 'Once upon a time: the development of sensitivity to story structure,' in C. Cooper, ed., *Researching Response to Literature and the Teaching of Literature: Points of Departure* (Norwood, New Jersey: Ablex, 1983).

16   Bruno Bettelheim, *The Uses of Enchantment: The Meaning and Importance of Fairy Tales* (New York: Vintage, 1977), Introduction.

17   J. B. Sykes, ed., *The Concise Oxford Dictionary of Current English* (New York and Oxford: Oxford University Press, 1976), p. 1136.

18   This list of story components and the subsequent story analysis were used in research reported by Stephanie H. McConaughy, 'Using story structure in the classroom,' *Language Arts* (February 1980), pp. 157-65.

Chapter 2: Should children still listen?

1   Robert P. Snow, *Creating Media Culture* (Beverly Hills: Sage, 1983), p. 99.

2   Marie Winn, 'Why has radio tuned out children?,' *The New York Times*, September 25, 1983.

3   Brian Brightly, then National Public Radio's Director of Educational Services, in Winn, 'Why has radio tuned out children?'

4   See, for example, Joel R. Levin and Alan M. Lesgold, 'On pictures in prose,' *Educational Communication and Technology Journal* (*26*, 3, 1978), pp. 233-43.

5   See Donald S. Hayes, Suzanne B. Kelly and Marcia Mandel, 'TV and radio contrasted: age differences in the retention of story events,' unpublished MS, University of Maine, 1983; Kathy Pezdek, Ariella Lehrer and S. Simon, 'The relationship between reading and cognitive processing of television and radio,' *Child Development* (*55*, 1984), pp. 2072-82; and Hertha Sturm and Sabine Jorg, *Information Processing by Young Children: Piaget's Theory of Intellectual Development Applied to Radio and Television* (Munich: Saur, 1981).

6   Gail E. Haley, *A Story a Story* (New York: Atheneum, 1970).

7   Eric Carle, *Eric Carle's Storybook: Seven Tales by the Brothers Grimm* (New York: Franklin Watts, 1976), p. 39.

8   Thomas J. Berndt and Emily G. Berndt, 'Children's use of motives and intentionality in person perception and moral judgment,' *Child Development* (*46*, 1975), pp. 904-12.

9   Jessica Beagles-Roos and Isabelle Gat, 'Specific impact of radio and television on children's story comprehension,' *Journal of Educational Psychology* (*75*, 1, 1983), pp. 128-37; and Martha M. Vibbert and Laurene K. Meringoff, 'Children's production and application of story imagery: a cross-medium investigation,' *ERIC Document* ED 210 682, 1981.

10   Ann L. Brown and Sandra S. Smiley, 'Rating the importance of structural units of prose passages: a problem of metacognitive development,' *Child Development* (*48*, 1977), pp. 1-8.

11   Jean Mandler and Nancy Johnson, 'Remembrance of things parsed: story structure and recall,' *Cognitive Psychology* (*9*, 1977), pp. 111-51.

12   Data collected for my unpublished EdD dissertation, 'A story a story: the influence of the medium on children's apprehension of stories,' Harvard University, 1978.

13   Susan R. Goldman and Connie Varnhagen, 'Comprehension of stories with no obstacle and obstacle endings,' *Child Development* (*54*, 1983), pp. 980-92.

14   Nancy L. Stein and Christine G. Glenn, 'An analysis of story comprehension in elementary school children,' in R. Freedle, ed., *New Directions in Discourse Processing*, vol. 2 (Hillsdale, New Jersey: Ablex, 1979); and Ray R. Buss *et al.*, 'Development of children's use of a story schema to retrieve information,' *Developmental Psychology* (*19*, 1, 1983), pp. 22-8.

15 Dorothy Poulsen, Eileen Kintsch and Walter Kintsch, 'Children's comprehension and memory for stories,' *Journal of Experimental Child Psychology* (*28*, 1979), pp. 379-403.

16 For pioneering studies on this subject, see Frederic C. Bartlett, *Remembering: A Study in Experimental and Social Psychology* (New York and Cambridge: Cambridge University Press, 1932).

17 Brown and Smiley, 'Rating the importance of structural units of prose passages.'

18 See discussion in Ruth Finnegan, *Oral Poetry: Its Nature, Significance, and Social Function* (New York and Cambridge: Cambridge University Press, 1977), chapter 4.

19 Shelley Rubin and Howard Gardner, 'Once upon a time: the development of sensitivity to story structure,' in C. Cooper, ed., *Researching Response to Literature and the Teaching of Literature: Points of Departure* (Norwood, New Jersey: Ablex, 1983).

20 Beagles-Roos and Gat, 'Specific impact of radio and television on children's story comprehension.'

21 Hayes, Kelly and Mandel, 'TV and radio contrasted.'

22 See Dennie Wolf, Sharon Grollman and William G. Scarlett, 'Kinds of text,' in D. Wolf and H. Gardner, eds, *The Making of Meanings*, submitted for publication.

23 Howard Gardner and William Lohman, 'Children's sensitivity to literary styles,' *Merrill-Palmer Quarterly* (*21*, 2, 1975), pp. 113-26; and Christine Massey *et al.*, 'Children's sensitivity to stylistic features in literature,' *Leonardo* (*16*, 3, 1983), pp. 204-7.

24 Cynthia A. Char, with Laurene K. Meringoff, 'Children's comprehension of radio stories and the role of sound effects and music in story comprehension,' Project Zero, Harvard University Graduate School of Education, Technical Report no. 28 (1982).

25 Vibbert and Meringoff, 'Children's production and application of story imagery.'

26 Gail S. Banker and Laurene K. Meringoff, 'Without words: the meaning children derive from a nonverbal film story,' *ERIC Document* ED 224 037, 1982.

27 Two authors who discuss the role of sound effects in producing effective radio drama are Rudolf Arnheim, *Radio: An Art of Sound*, 2nd edn (New York: DaCapo, 1972); and Tony Schwartz, *The Responsive Chord* (Garden City, New York: Doubleday, 1974).

28 Elwyn Evans, *Radio: A Guide to Broadcasting Techniques* (Levittown, New York: Transatlantic Arts, 1977), p.133.

29   Char with Meringoff, 'Children's comprehension of radio stories.'

30   Ibid.

31   Hsing-Wu Chang and Sandra E. Trehub, 'Auditory processing of relational information by young infants,' *Journal of Experimental Child Psychology* (24, 1977), pp. 324-31; and Hsing-Wu Chang and Sandra E. Trehub, 'Infants' perception of temporal grouping in auditory patterns,' *Child Development* (48, 1977), pp. 1666-70.

32   Char with Meringoff, 'Children's comprehension of radio stories.'

33   See discussion in Steven Seidman, 'On the contributions of music to media productions,' *Educational Communication and Technology Journal* (29, 1, 1981), pp. 49-61.

34   Char with Meringoff, 'Children's comprehension of radio stories.'

35   Seidman, 'On the contributions of music to media productions.'

36   See discussion in Jim Trelease, *The Read-Aloud Handbook* (New York: Penguin, 1982), chapters 1 and 2. For more information, see Sandra McCormick, 'Should you read aloud to your children?,' *Language Arts* (February 1977), pp. 139-43.

37   Kathy Pezdek and Ariella Lehrer, 'The relationship between reading and cognitive processing of television and radio.'

38   A. Hildyard and David R. Olson, 'Memory and inference in comprehension of oral and written discourse,' *Discourse Processes* (1, 2, 1978), pp. 91-117.

39   Herbert A. Leeper and Cheryl L. Thomas, 'Young children's preferences for listening rates,' *Perceptual and Motor Skills* (47, 1978), pp. 891-8.

40   Walter Kintsch and Ely Kozminsky, 'Summarizing stories after reading and listening,' *Journal of Educational Psychology* (69, 5, 1977), pp. 491-9.

41   For an impassioned argument for exposing children to the best literature see Bruno Bettelheim and Karen Zelan, *On Learning to Read: The Child's Fascination with Meaning* (New York: Knopf, 1982).

42   Alden J. Moe, 'Using picture books for reading vocabulary development,' in J. W. Stewig and S. L. Sebesta, eds, *Using Literature in the Elementary Classroom* (Urbana, Ill.: National Council of Teachers of English, 1978).

43   Terence McNally in Samuel G. Freedman, 'For McNally, a new show and an old struggle,' *The New York Times*, February 5, 1984.

Chapter 3: Why read children picture books?

1   See discussion in Jim Trelease, *The Read-Aloud Handbook* (New York: Penguin, 1982), chapters 1 and 2.

2   S. Jay Samuels, 'Effects of pictures on learning to read, comprehension, and attitudes,' *Review of Educational Research* (40, 1970), pp. 397-407.

3   Dale M. Willows, 'A picture is not always worth a thousand words: pictures as distractors in reading,' *Journal of Educational Psychology* (70, 2, 1978), pp. 255-62.

4   That statements cannot be expressed in pictures is discussed by E. H. Gombrich, 'The visual image,' in D. R. Olson, ed., *Media and Symbols: The Forms of Expression, Communication, and Education* (Chicago: National Society for the Study of Education, 1974),p. 243.

5   J. Peeck, 'Retention of pictorial and verbal content of a text with illustrations,' *Journal of Educational Psychology* (66, 1974), pp. 880-8.

6   Bruno Bettelheim, *The Uses of Enchantment: The Meaning and Importance of Fairy Tales* (New York: Vintage, 1977), p. 60.

7   Lewis Carroll, *The Annotated Alice: Alice's Adventures in Wonderland and Through the Looking Glass* (Cleveland and New York: World, 1963), p. 25.

8   S. Jay Samuels, Edieann Biesbrock and Pamela R. Terry, 'The effect of pictures on children's attitudes toward presented stories,' *Journal of Educational Research* (67, 6, 1974), pp. 243-6.

9   Joel R. Levin and Alan M. Lesgold, 'On pictures in prose,' *Educational Communication and Technology Journal* (26, 3, 1978), pp. 233-43.

10   See discussion in Diane Lemonnier Schallert, 'The role of illustrations in reading comprehension,' in R. J. Spiro, B. C. Bruce and W. F. Brewer, eds, *Theoretical Issues in Reading Comprehension: Perspectives from Cognitive Psychology, Linguistics, Artificial Intelligence, and Education* (Hillsdale, New Jersey: Lawrence Erlbaum, 1981).

11   Joel R. Levin, B. G. Bender and Alan M. Lesgold, 'Pictures, repetition, and young children's oral prose learning,' *AV Communications Review* (24, 1976), pp. 367-80.

12   Peeck, 'Retention of pictorial and verbal content of a text with illustrations.'

13   Cynthia A. Char, with Laurene K. Meringoff, 'The role of story illustrations: children's story comprehension in three different media,' Project Zero, Harvard University Graduate School of Education, Technical Report no. 22 (1981).

14   David E. Campbell and Toni A. Campbell, 'Effects of live and

recorded storytelling on retelling performance of preschool children from low socioeconomic backgrounds,' *Psychology in the Schools* (13, 2, 1976), pp. 201-4.

15 Comparing the live reading in Laurene Krasny Meringoff, 'Influence of the medium on children's story apprehension,' *Journal of Educational Psychology* (72, 2, 1980), pp. 240-9 with the recorded narration in Char, with Meringoff, 'The role of story illustrations,' p. 18.

16 Meringoff, 'Influence of the medium on children's story apprehension.'

17 Hope Kelly and Laurene K. Meringoff, 'Television and books: a comparison of story comprehension in two media,' paper presented at the Annual Convention of the American Psychological Association, New York City, September 1979.

18 For research on toddler-parent conversation centered around television viewing, see Dafna Lemish and Mabel Rice, 'Toddlers, talk and television: observations in the home,' paper presented at the International Communication Association Convention, San Francisco, May 1984.

19 Catherine E. Snow and Beverly A. Goldfield, 'Building stories: the emergence of information structures from conversation,' in D. Tannen, ed., *Analyzing Discourse: Text and Talk* (Georgetown, Virginia: Georgetown University Press, 1981).

21 See, for example, Carol Chomsky, 'Stages in language development and reading exposure,' *Harvard Educational Review* (42, 1972), pp. 1-33; and Sandra McCormick, 'Should you read aloud to your children?,' *Language Arts* (February 1977), pp. 139-44.

21 Trelease, *The Read-Aloud Handbook*, p. 26.

22 Laura Simms, 'Storytelling, children, and imagination,' *Texas Library Journal* (Winter 1981), pp. 110-12. Also see Laura Simms, 'Words in our hearts: the experience of the story,' *The Horn Book Magazine* (June 1983), pp. 344-7.

Chapter 4: Children's illustration preferences

1 Howard Gardner, 'Children's perceptions of works of art: a developmental portrait,' in D. O'Hare, ed., *Psychology and the Arts* (Hassocks, Sussex: Harvester Press, 1981); and Michael Parsons, Marilyn Johnston and Robert Durham, 'Developmental stages in children's aesthetic responses,' *Journal of Aesthetic Education* (12, 1, 1978), pp.83-104.

2 See J. DeLoache, M. Strauss and J. Maynard, 'Picture perception in infancy,' *Infant Behavior and Development* (2, 1979), pp. 77-89.

3 Betty Lark-Horowitz, 'On art appreciation of children: portrait preference study,' *Journal of Educational Research (31*, 8, 1938), pp. 572-98; and Anne K. Rosenstiel *et al.*, 'Critical judgment: a developmental study,' *Journal of Aesthetic Education (12*, 4, 1978), pp. 95-107.

4 Gardner, 'Children's perceptions of works of art;' Parsons *et al.*, 'Developmental stages in children's aesthetic responses;' Rosenstiel *et al.*, 'Critical judgment.'

5 See also review of research in Ellen Winner, *Invented Worlds: The Psychology of the Arts* (Cambridge, Mass.: Harvard University Press, 1983), pp. 140-3.

6 Howard Gardner, 'Children's sensitivity to painting styles,' *Child Development (41*, 1970), pp. 813-21.

7 Paula Blank *et al.*, 'Perceiving what paintings express,' in W. R. Crozier and A. Chapman, eds, *Cognitive Processes in the Perception of Art* (Amsterdam: North Holland Press, 1984).

8 Winner, *Invented Worlds*, p. 139.

9 See Stephen M. Kosslyn, Karen H. Heldmeyer and Eileen P. Locklear, 'Children's drawings as data about internal representations,' *Journal of Experimental Child Psychology (23*, 1977), pp. 191-211.

10 Winner, *Invented Worlds*, p. 129.

11 Gardner, 'Children's sensitivity to painting styles;' and Abigail Housen, 'The eye of the beholder: measuring aesthetic development,' unpublished EdD dissertation, Harvard University, 1983.

12 Lark-Horowitz, 'On art appreciation of children.'

13 John J. McKendry, ed., *Aesop: Five Centuries of Illustrated Fables* (New York: Metropolitan Museum of Art, 1964). p. 5.

14 Text adapted from Anne Terry White, *Aesop Fables*, (New York: Random House, 1964).

Chapter 5: No, but I saw the movie

1 See Sarah L. Friedman and Marguerite B. Stevenson, 'Developmental changes in the understanding of implied motion in two-dimensional pictures,' *Child Development (48*, 1975), pp. 773-8.

2 Laurene Krasny Meringoff, 'Influence of the medium on children's story apprehension,' *Journal of Educational Psychology (72*, 2, 1980), pp. 240-9.

3 Gene Deitch, 'The picture book animated,' *The Horn Book Magazine* (April 1978), p. 146.

4 Donald S. Hayes, Suzanne B. Kelly and Marcia Mandel, 'TV and radio contrasted: age differences in the retention of story events,' unpublished MS, University of Maine, 1983.

5 Patricia M. Greenfield, personal communication, January 1984.

6 Donald S. Hayes and Suzanne B. Kelly, 'Young children's processing of television: modality differences in the integration of temporal and cause-effect relations,' *Journal of Experimental Child Psychology* (*38*, 1984), pp. 505-14.

7 Sandra L. Calvert *et al.*, 'The relation between selective attention to television forms and children's comprehension of content,' *Child Development* (*53*, 1982), pp. 601-10.

8 Aletha C. Huston and John C. Wright, 'Children's processing of television: the informative functions of formal features,' in J. Bryant and D. R. Anderson, eds, *Children's Understanding of Television: Research on Attention and Comprehension* (New York: Academic Press, 1983); and Steven Levin and Daniel R. Anderson, 'The development of attention,' *Journal of Communication* (*26*, 2, 1976), pp. 126-35.

9 Huston and Wright, 'Children's processing of television.'

10 Kathy Pezdek and Ellen Stevens, 'Children's memory for auditory and visual information on television,' *Developmental Psychology* (*20*, 1984), pp. 212-18.

11 For two thoughtful discussions comparing media, see George Bluestone, *Novels into Film: The Metamorphosis of Fiction into Cinema* (Berkeley: University of California Press, 1973); and Seymour Chatman, 'What novels can do that films can't (and vice versa),' *Critical Inquiry* (*7*, 1, 1980), pp. 121-40.

12 For a technical analysis of film, see James Monaco, *How to Read a Film* (New York and Oxford: Oxford University Press, 1977). For a conceptual analysis, see Søren Kjørup, 'Film as a meetingplace of multiple codes,' in D. Perkins and B. Leondar, eds, *The Arts and Cognition* (Baltimore: Johns Hopkins University Press, 1977).

13 See Randall P. Harrison, *The Cartoon: Communication to the Quick* (Beverly Hills: Sage, 1981).

14 John Gardner, *The Art of Fiction* (New York: Knopf, 1984), p. 111.

15 Chatman, 'What novels can do that films can't (and vice versa).'

16 Gail S. Banker and Laurene K. Meringoff, 'Without words: the meaning children derive from a nonverbal film story,' *ERIC Document* ED 224 037, 1982; Jessica Beagles-Roos and Isabelle Gat, 'Specific impact of radio and television on children's story comprehension,' *Journal of*

Educational Psychology (75, 1, 1983), pp. 128-37; and Martha M. Vibbert and Laurene K. Meringoff, 'Children's production and application of story imagery: a cross-medium investigation,' *ERIC Document* ED 210 682, 1981.

17   Hope Kelly and Laurene K. Meringoff, 'A comparison of story comprehension in two media: books and television,' paper presented at the Annual Convention of the American Psychological Association, New York City, September 1979; and Meringoff, 'Influence of the medium on children's story apprehension.'

18   Meringoff, ibid.

19   This example and the following one are from Vibbert and Meringoff, 'Children's production and application of story imagery.'

20   Laurene Krasny Meringoff, 'A story a story: the influence of the medium on children's apprehension of stories,' unpublished EdD dissertation, Harvard University, 1978.

21   See Aimee Dorr, Catherine Doubleday and Peter Kovariac, 'Emotions depicted on and stimulated by television programs,' in M. Meyer, ed., *Children and the Formal Features of Television* (Munich: Saur, 1983); and Ann Knowles and Mary Nixon, 'Young children's understanding of emotional states as depicted by television cartoon characters,' Monash University, monograph (1983).

22   Dorr, Doubleday and Kovariac, 'Emotions depicted on and stimulated by television programs;' and Lisa Reichenbach and John C. Masters, 'Children's use of expressive and contextual cues in judgments of emotion,' *Child Development* (54, 1983), pp. 993-1004.

23   This study is summarized in Kelly and Meringoff, 'A comparison of story comprehension in two media.'

24   Morton Schindel, producer, *The Three Robbers* (Weston, Conn.: Weston Woods, 1972), film. For the picture book, see Tomi Ungerer, *The Three Robbers* (New York: Atheneum, 1962).

25   Dorothy Flapan, *Children's Understanding of Social Interaction* (New York: Teachers College Press, 1968).

26   Stephen R. Acker and Robert K. Tiemens, 'Children's perceptions of changes in size of televised images,' *Human Communication Research* (7, 4, 1981), pp. 340-6.

27   Stephen R. Acker, 'Speed, space, kids and the television cyclops: viewers' perceptions of velocity and distance in televised events,' *Human Communication Research* (Summer 1983).

28   Karel Reisz and Gavin Millar, *The Technique of Film Editing*, 2nd edn

(New York: Hastings House, 1968), p. 216.

29 Data collected for Kelly and Meringoff, 'A comparison of story comprehension in two media.'

30 Banker and Meringoff, 'Without words.' Also data collected for Kelly and Meringoff, 'A comparison of story comprehension in two media,' and Meringoff, 'Influence of the medium on children's story apprehension.'

31 See Paul Fraisse, 'The adaptation of the child to time,' in W. J. Friedman, ed., *The Developmental Psychology of Time* (New York: Academic Press, 1982).

32 W. Andrew Collins, 'Interpretation and inference in children's television viewing,' in J. Bryant and D. R. Anderson, eds, *Children's Understanding of Television: Research on Attention and Comprehension* (New York: Academic Press, 1983).

33 See review in Robert Hornik, 'Out-of-school television and schooling: hypotheses and methods,' *Review of Educational Research* (51, 2, 1981), pp. 193-214.

34 Hilde T. Himmelweit, A. N. Oppenheim and Pamela Vince, *Television and the Child: An Empirical Study of the Effects of Television on the Young* (New York and Oxford: Oxford University Press, 1958).

35 See, for example, V. Greaney, 'Factors related to amount and type of leisure time reading,' *Reading Research Quarterly* (15, 1980), pp. 337-57; and Hornik, 'Out-of-school television and schooling.'

36 See discussion in Gavriel Salomon, 'Television literacy and television vs. literacy,' paper presented at the Conference on Literacy in the 1980s, University of Michigan, June 1981.

37 See Harlan Hamilton, 'TV tie-ins as a bridge to books,' *Language Arts* (February 1976), pp. 129-31; and John E. Splaine, 'Television and its influence on reading,' *Educational Technology* (June 1978), pp. 15-19.

38 Susan B. Neuman, 'Television viewing and leisure reading: a qualitative analysis,' *Journal of Educational Research* (75, 5, 1982), pp. 299-304.

39 Support for this speculation comes from a study reporting more TV-oriented reading among heavy than light viewers. See Michael Morgan and Larry Gross, 'Television viewing, IQ, and academic achievement,' *Journal of Broadcasting* (30, 1, 1980), pp. 117-33.

40 For an interesting interpretation of these books' popularity, see Janet Maslin, 'Readers may look to books for what's not on screen,' *The New York Times*, August 7, 1983.

41   For reviews of research, see Hornik, 'Out-of-school television and schooling;' Susan B. Neuman, 'Television: its effects on reading and school achievement,' *The Reading Teacher* (April 1980), pp. 801-5; and David Pearl, *Television and Behavior: Ten Years of Scientific Progress and Implications for the Eighties: Summary Report* (Washington, DC: National Institute of Mental Health, 1982), pp. 79-86.

42   Donald F. Roberts *et al.*, 'Reading and television predictors of reading achievement at different age levels,' *Communication Research* (11, 1, 1984), p. 9-49.

Chapter 6: Does television stifle imagination?

1   Bruce Watkins *et al.*, 'Children's use of TV and real-life story structure and content as a function of age and prime-time television viewing,' *First Annual Report to the Spencer Foundation* (Ann Arbor: University of Michigan, 1981).

2   Laurene K. Meringoff, 'Viewpoints,' *Language Arts* (March 1981), pp. 281-2.

3   But perhaps the investments are not as formidable as we fear. For suggestions, see Kit Laybourne and Pauline Cianciolo, eds, *Doing the Media* (New York: McGraw-Hill, 1978), Part 3, Film and Part 4, Video; and Charles D. Gaitskell and Al Hurwitz, *Children and Their Art: Methods for the Elementary School*, 3rd edn (New York: Harcourt Brace Jovanovich, 1975), pp. 297-313.

4   Stephen M. Kosslyn, Karen H. Heldmeyer and Eileen P. Locklear, 'Children's drawings as data about internal representations,' *Journal of Experimental Child Psychology* (23, 1977), pp. 191-211.

5   Thomas Carothers and Howard Gardner, 'When children's drawings become art: the emergence of aesthetic production and perception,' *Developmental Psychology* (15, 5, 1979), pp. 570-80.

6   Koslyn *et al.*, 'Children's drawings as data about internal representations.'

7   See Claire Golomb, 'The child as image-maker: the invention of representational models and the effects of the medium,' *Studies in Art Education* (17, 2, 1977), pp. 19-27.

8   Howard Gardner, *Artful Scribbles: The Significance of Children's Drawings* (New York: Basic Books, 1980), chapter 6.

9   Golomb, 'The child as image-maker.'

10   Rudolf Arnheim, *Art and Visual Perception* (Berkeley: University of California Press, 1974), chapter 4.

11   For an insightful look at the critical judgments adult artists make, see David N. Perkins, *The Mind's Best Work* (Cambridge, Mass.: Harvard University Press, 1981), pp. 126-9.

12   Jeffrey L. Hartley *et al.*, 'Abstraction of individual styles from the drawings of 5-year-old children,' *Child Development* (53, 1982). pp. 1193-214.

13   S. J. Phillips, producer, *The Fisherman and His Wife* (Santa Monica: Bosustow Productions, 1977). This animated film appeared on broadcast television in Massachusetts during the school day.

14   This study was conducted by Laurene K. Meringoff and Martha M. Vibbert with the help of Boston area public school children. The research appears in Laurene K. Meringoff *et al.*, 'How is children's learning from television distinctive? Exploiting the medium methodologically,' in J. Bryant and D. R. Anderson, eds, *Children's Understanding of Television: Research on Attention and Comprehension* (New York: Academic Press, 1983), pp. 151-79. A Technical Report by Vibbert and Meringoff describing the study details is *ERIC Document* ED 210 682 1981.

15   Arnheim, *Art and Visual Perception*.

16   William Ives and Joanne Rovet, 'The role of graphic orientations in children's drawings of familiar and novel objects at rest and in motion,' *Merrill-Palmer Quarterly* (25, 1979), pp. 281-92. For developmental stages in drawing, also see Jacqueline Goodnow, *Children Drawing* (Cambridge, Mass.: Harvard University Press, 1977).

17   Paul E. Torrance, 'Tendency to produce unusual visual perspective as a predictor of creative achievement,' *Perceptual and Motor Skills* (34, 1972), pp. 911-15.

18   See text in *The Complete Grimms' Fairy Tales*, ill. by Pauline Allison (London and Boston: Routledge & Kegan Paul, 1981).

19   Martin S. Lindauer, 'Imagery and sensory modality,' *Perceptual and Motor Skills* (29, 1969), pp. 203-15.

20   See, for example, Jerome L. Singer and Dorothy G. Singer, *Television, Imagination and Aggression: A Study of Preschoolers* (Hillsdale, New Jersey: Erlbaum, 1981). For continuation of study and final data, see Jerome L. Singer, Dorothy G. Singer and Wanda Rapaczynski, 'Children's imagination as predicted by family patterns and television viewing: a longitudinal study,' *Genetic Psychology Monographs*, 110 (August 1984), pp. 43-69.

21   Caroline W. Meline, 'Does the medium matter?,' *Journal of Communication* (26, 3, 1976), pp.81-9.

22   Lecoq De Boisbaudran, *The Training of the Memory in Art and the*

Education of the Artist (London: Macmillan, 1914), p. 21.

23   See studies by Judith M. Burton, 'Representing experience from imagination and observation,' *School Arts* (December 1980), pp. 26-30; and David Pariser, reported in Gardner, *Artful Scribbles*, pp. 164-6.

24   See Brent Wilson and Majorie Wilson, 'An iconoclastic view of the imagery sources in the drawings of young people,' *Art Education* (January 1977), pp. 5-17.

25   See discussion in Gardner, *Artful Scribbles*, pp. 164-91.

26   See critique by John Corry, 'Cartoons or commercials?,' *The New York Times*, October 30, 1983.

Chapter 7: Choosing heroes and heroines

1   See P. L. Travers, 'The world of the hero,' *Parabola* (1, 1, 1976), pp. 42-7.

2   For a fascinating and thorough analysis of Russian fairy tales, see Vladimir Propp, *Morphology of the Folktale*, 2nd edn (Austin, Texas: University of Texas Press, 1968). By Propp's count, a total of thirty-one different kinds of character actions comprise the fairy tales.

3   See the eloquent discussion of this broader definition in Northrop Frye, *Anatomy of Criticism*, (Princeton, New Jersey: Princeton University Press, 1957), pp. 33-52.

4   For an historical analysis of how this operates for children's media in France, see Marie-Jose Chombart de Lauwe and Claude Bellan, *Enfants de L'Image* (Children of the Image) (Paris: Payot, 1979).

5   Laurence Sterne, *Tristram Shandy*, vol. 2 (New York: Pocket Library, 1957), p. 83.

6   The notion of fiction's 'secondary world' is described by J. R. R. Tolkien, 'On fairy-stories,' in *Tree and Leaf* (London: Unwin Books, 1964), p. 36. Reversals of narrative ground rules in fantasy are discussed in Eric Rabkin, *The Fantastic in Literature* (Princeton, New Jersey: Princeton University Press, 1976).

7   For an elaboration of this active view of audience members, see Norman N. Holland, *The Dynamics of Literary Response* (New York: W. W. Norton, 1975).

8   Reported in Arthur N. Applebee, *The Child's Concept of Story: Ages 2-17* (Chicago: University of Chicago Press, 1978), chapter 5.

9   See, for example, Eleanor Maccoby and William C. Wilson, 'Identification and observational learning from films,' *Journal of Abnormal and Social Psychology* (55,1957), pp. 76-87.

10   David E. Fernie, 'Ordinary and extraordinary people: children's understanding of television and real life models,' in H. Kelly and H. Gardner, eds, *New Directions for Child Development: Viewing Children Through Television*, no. 13 (San Francisco: Jossey-Bass, 1981), pp. 47-58.

11   See Shari Robinson, David E. Fernie and Laurene K. Meringoff, 'Heroes, humbugs, and also-rans: children's preferences and evaluations concerning television characters,' *ERIC Document* ED 223 329, 1982.

12   'On and off the avenue: on, Comet! on, Cupid! on, Donder and Blitzen!,' *The New Yorker*, December 12, 1983, p. 126.

13   See M. M. Miller and Byron Reeves, 'Dramatic TV content and children's sex-role stereotypes,' *Journal of Broadcasting* (20, 1976), pp. 35-50.

14   See Bruno Bettelheim, *The Uses of Enchantment: The Meaning and Importance of Fairy Tales* (New York: Vintage, 1977).

15   David E. Fernie, 'Ordinary and extraordinary people.'

16   See Aimee Dorr, 'No shortcuts to judging reality,' in J. Bryant and D. R. Anderson, eds, *Children's Understanding of Television: Research on Attention and Comprehension* (New York: Academic Press, 1983); and Patricia Morison and Howard Gardner, 'Dragons and dinosaurs: the child's capacity to differentiate fantasy from reality,' *Child Development* (49, 1978), pp. 642-8.

17   Laura Simms and Bill Kough, eds, Students of P.S. 87: *Paint a Picture in Your Mind* (New York: Teachers' and Writers' Collaborative, 1981).

18   Daniel R. Anderson, 'Watching children watch television,' in G. Hale and M. Lewis, eds, *Attention and the Development of Cognitive Skills* (New York: Plenum, 1979).

19   Leona Jaglom and Howard Gardner, 'Decoding the worlds of television,' *Studies in Visual Communication* (7, 1981), pp. 33-47.

20   David Pearl, Project Director, *Television and Behavior: Ten Years of Scientific Progress and Implications for the Eighties: Summary Report* (Rockville, Maryland: National Institute of Mental Health, 1982), pp. 36-8.

21   Brian Coates, H. Ellison Pusser and Irene Goodman, 'The influence of Sesame Street and Mister Rogers' Neighborhood on children's social behavior in the preschool,' *Child Development* (47, 1976), pp. 138-44; Jerry L. Fryear and Mark H. Thelen, 'Effect of sex of model and sex of observer on the imitation of affectionate behavior,' *Developmental Psychology* (1, 1969), p. 298; and Lynette K. Friedrich and Aletha H. Stein, 'Aggressive and prosocial television programs and the natural behavior of preschool children,' *Monographs of the Society for Research in Child Development*, no.

151 (*38*, 4, 1973).

22   I. M. Ahammer and John P. Murray, 'Kindness in the kindergarten: the relative influence of role playing and prosocial television in facilitating altruism,' *International Journal of Behavioral Development* (2,1979), pp. 133-57; and Joyce M. Sprafkin, Robert M. Liebert and Rita W. Poulos, 'Effects of a prosocial example on children's helping,' *Journal of Experimental Child Psychology* (*20*, 1975), pp. 119-26.

23   Gerald M. Stein and James H. Bryan, 'The effects of a televised model upon rule adoption behavior of children,' *Child Development* (*43*, 1972), pp. 268-73; and Thomas M. Wolf and J. Allan Cheyne, 'Persistence of effects of live behavioral, televised behavioral, and live verbal models on resistance to deviation,' *Child Development* (*43*, 1972), pp. 1429-1436.

24   For discussion of the conditions for observational learning, see Albert Bandura, *Social Learning Theory* (New York: Prentice-Hall, 1977).

25   Grant Noble, 'Social learning from everyday television,' in M. Howe, ed., *Learning from Television: Psychological and Educational Research* (London: Academic Press, 1983).

26   Robinson *et al.*, 'Heroes, humbug, and also-rans.'

27   Another explanation for these books' popularity criticizes recent movies for their underdeveloped plots and characters, which leave viewers still hungry for more. See Janet Maslin, 'Readers may look to books for what's not on the screen,' *The New York Times*, August 7, 1983.

28   Dafna Lemish and Mabel Rice, 'Toddlers, talk and television,' paper presented at the International Communication Association Convention, San Francisco, May 1984.

Chapter 8: When computers get into the storytelling act

1   For information on video cassette recorders as products for home use, see David Lachenbruch, 'The VCR is changing the whole TV picture,' *Channels*, March 1984, p. 16; and David Lachenbruch, 'VCRs: the hottest thing since television,' *Channels*, Field Guide 1985, pp. 6, 8.

2   For a quick rundown on how a computer works and what its components can do, read Carol and Herbert Klitzner, *Help Your Child Succeed With a Computer* (New York: Simon & Schuster, 1984), pp. 35-76.

3   Computer program screen from Milton Bradley, *Vocabulary Skills: Context Clues* (Baltimore, Maryland: Media Materials, 1982).

4   For probing discussions of computer-assisted instruction see Jan Hawkins, 'The flexible use of computers in classrooms,' Center for

Children and Technology, Bank Street College of Education, Technical Report no. 6 (1982); and Judah Schwartz, 'Tyranny, discipline, freedom, license: some thoughts on educational ideology and computers,' *Education in the Electronic Age* (New York: WNET Learning Lab/Educational Broadcasting Corp., 1983).

5 See Steven Levy, 'Fantastic worlds of the computer game,' *Channels*, November 1983, pp. 6-9.

6 Following widespread publicity and a politician's protest, a British company withdrew an objectionable video game in which British submarines torpedo Argentine warships. See Reuters New Service story in *The New York Times*, April 11, 1984.

7 Diana Gagnon, 'Videogames and spatial skills: a pilot study,' *Educational Communication and Technology Journal* (1985, in press). Also see discussion in Patricia Marks Greenfield, *Mind and Media* (Cambridge, Mass.: Harvard University Press, 1984), chapter 7.

8 Gagnon, 'Videogames and spatial skills.'

9 See discussion in Howard Gardner, *Frames of Mind: The Theory of Multiple Intelligences* (New York: Basic Books, 1983), chapter 8.

10 The computer program, *Swiss Family Robinson*, is based on the book, *The Swiss Family Robinson*, by Johann Wyss, which was originally published in the eighteenth century. Program developed by Tom Snyder Productions (Cambridge, Mass.: Windham Classics, 1984).

11 A screen from *Swiss Family Robinson*.

12 Computer program screen from Learningways, *MasterType's Writing Wizard* (Tarrytown, New York: Scarborough Systems, 1984).

13 See discussion in Karen Sheingold, Jan Hawkins and D. Midian Kurland, 'Classroom software for the information age,' Center for Children and Technology, Bank Street College of Education, Technical Report no. 23 (1983).

14 In an enthusiastic report, third through fifth graders use a word processor to produce a monthly newspaper. See James A. Levin and Marcia J. Boruta, 'Writing with computers in classrooms: "You get exactly the right amount of space!",' *Theory Into Practice* (22, 4, 1983), pp. 291-5. Also see Jan Hawkins *et al.*, 'Microcomputers in schools: impact on the social life of elementary classrooms,' *Journal of Applied Developmental Psychology* (3, 1982), pp. 361-73.

15 See James A. Levin *et al.*, 'Muktuk meets Jacuzzi: computer networks and elementary school writers,' in S. W. Freedman, ed., *The Acquisition of Written Language: Revision and Response* (Hillsdale, New Jersey: Ablex, 1984).

16   Levin, *et al.*, 'Muktuk meets Jacuzzi.'

17   Janet H. Kane, 'Computers for composing,' Center for Children and Technology, Bank Street College of Education, Technical Report no. 21 (1983).

18   Kane, 'Computers for composing.'

19   See Colette Daiute and John Kruidenier, 'A self-questioning strategy to increase young writers' revising processes,' *Journal of Applied Psycholinguistics* (1985, in press); and Levin *et al.*, 'Muktuk meets Jacuzzi.'

20   For information about using computer-based text analysis and error identification with children, see Colette Daiute, 'Computers and the teaching of writing,' in D. Peterson, ed., *Intelligent Schoolhouse* (Reston, Virginia: Reston Publishing, 1984). For summary of evaluation for a computer writing program tested in third through fifth grade classrooms and introduced with teachers' help, see Andee Rubin and Bertram Bruce, 'Learning with QUILL: lessons for students, teachers, and software designers,' in T. E. Raphael and R. E. Reynolds, eds, *Contexts of Literacy* (New York: Longman, 1985). Another approach to writing I have seen work effectively in the Farrell, Pennsylvania schools is to have children submit their work to an anonymous editor and receive feedback, both via computer.

21   LOGO is described in Seymour Papert, *Mindstorms: Children, Computers, and Powerful Ideas* (New York: Basic Books, 1980).

22   Sheila Vaidya and John McKeeby, 'Computer turtle graphics: do they affect children's thought processes?,' *Educational Technology* (September 1984), pp. 46-7.

23   Sherry Turkle, *The Second Self: Computers and the Human Spirit* (New York: Simon & Schuster, 1984), p. 30.

24   See Carolyn Marvin and Mark Winther, 'Computer-ease: a twentieth-century literacy emergent,' *Journal of Communication* (Winter 1983), pp.92-108. Also see Roy D. Pea and D. Midian Kurland, 'On the cognitive effects of learning computer programming: a critical look,' Center for Children and Technology, Bank Street College of Education, Technical Report no. 9 (1984).

25   See Henry M. Levin and Russell W. Rumberger, 'The educational implications of high technology,' Institute for Research on Educational Finance and Governance, Stanford University School of Education, Project Report no. 83 A4 (1983).

26   See discussion in Papert, *Mindstorms*. Also see critical discussion in Pea and Kurland, 'On the cognitive effects of learning computer programming.'

27   Gavriel Salomon and Howard Gardner discuss computers in terms of their versatile symbolic use in 'The computer as educator: lessons from television research,' unpublished MS, Project Zero, Harvard University, 1984.

Index